PETER HENRICI, S.J.

A PRACTICAL GUIDE TO STUDY

With a bibliography of tools of work
for Philosophy and Theology

Translated
by
Ivo Coelho, SDB

Original: P. Henrici, *Guida pratica allo studio. Con una bibliografia degli strumenti di lavoro per la Filosofia e la Teologia.* Third revised edition. Rome: Editrice Pontificia Università Gregoriana; 1992

Roma
2004

ISBN 88-7652-983-7

EDITRICE PONTIFICIA UNIVERSITÀ GREGORIANA
Piazza della Pilotta, 35 - 00187 Roma, Italia

INTRODUCTION

There is no dearth of manuals of methodology, even in the areas of philosophy and theology. But these are normally meant for advanced students who are about to begin research on their doctoral thesis. The ones instead who really need a helping hand are the students who come out of high school and find in the University a method which is quite different from the one they were used to: no more daily homework, no dialogue between professors and students, but instead courses, lectures and seminars which, though seeming to leave the students passive, actually call for a greater and a more personal effort of assimilation.

Our methodological counsels are therefore directed in the first place to beginners, with the aim of helping them overcome the initial consternation and of making their study more profitable from the very beginning. However, some of the bibliographical indications and techniques of research described within certainly go beyond the needs and even the capacities of a beginner, for we would like that this methodological "primer" be useful also to the more advanced student.

The points made here are meant to be assimilated not so much through private reading but through the practical exercises of a "proseminar" done under the guidance of an expert. The professor should make sure that every now and then he or she applies the purely formal "practical exercises" suggested at the end of each chapter to the particular matter which the students have in hand.

A methodology of study always presupposes a didactical theory. It will be seen that our theory is far from being innovative, being founded on the traditional distinction between courses, manuals and seminars. This is not so much for the sake of accommodating ourselves to the present state of affairs, but because we believe that this method of teaching, enlivened from within, is still capable of giving excellent results.

With the intention of covering the whole range of university studies, a Fifth Part on the doctoral thesis has been added to the present third edition, which has also been completely revised and updated as far as the bibliographies are concerned. Because of this, it has been possible to remove from the chapter on the licentiate dissertation certain counsels which were neither suitable nor necessary to that level of study. Again, it will be evident that our "practical guide" will not be able to expose all the methodological principles necessary for doctoral research; it seeks rather to give a helping hand with regard to the difficulties which doctoral students encounter in their work. Finally, there has been added a chapter on a new instrument of work which is especially useful in the redaction of a doctoral thesis: the personal computer. For this chapter I am indebted to Fr. Paul Gilbert.

Besides him, I would like to thank several colleagues and assistants for their advice and suggestions, and in the first place Fr. Carlo Huber, co-author of the Latin notes of which the present pages are a re-elaboration.

THE PROCESS

Initial openness. No one is born alone and no one grows without nourishment. The baby receives everything from others - life, food, language, customs - but transforms all this into something that is unmistakably original: his or her personality. The same can be said with regard to knowing: we never start from scratch, we never construct by ourselves the whole of knowledge; each one of us receives a "traditional" knowledge already constituted by others. This knowledge, however, must be *assimilated* in a way that is all our own, making of it *our* knowledge.

Clearly then the first step and the foundation of all study is an openness that is able to assimilate.

The effort to understand. It is not enough to swallow food; one must also digest it. Only then does it become nourishing.

The only result of a purely receptive attitude in study would be the burdening of the memory with useless information (notionism). One must "digest" what has been taught; one must make the effort to *understand* it, with the intention of *appropriating* it. One should be able to say, "I know", and not merely, "The master says". Take for example the study of mathematics: merely "believing" the theorem of Pythagoras does not amount to knowing the theorem; one knows the theorem only if one is able to "demonstrate" it.

Therefore every study, even assimilative study, is necessarily *active.*

The peculiarity of university study. It is taken for granted that the university student is mature enough to be able to *assimilate* what he is taught. In elementary and middle school, such assimilation is aided by means of constant inter-action between teacher and students. At the level of the uni-versity instead, the matter is simply *offered* to the students, and it is up to each student to make the effort to *assimilate* it actively. That is why the university student may *seem* more passive and more purely receptive than the high school stu-dent; in point of fact instead, he is expected to be *more responsible* and involved.

Introduction to creative work. At the university level, it is a question of the formation not so much of good disciples as of *future masters* who will hand on to others, in one way or another, what they themselves have learnt. That is why active study is so much the more essential, because it consti-tutes an introduction and a *training to such future activity –* which will nevertheless always remain a type of "study", because it will continue to be a question of taking up and extending a knowledge that is already constituted. The chief tools in this introduction to creative study are the *seminars* and the *dissertations* required for the higher academic degrees.

These notes will follow the dynamism of study itself, describing first the usual *teaching methods*, and then the *work demanded of the student*, beginning from receptive study to work that is more properly creative.

BIBLIOGRAPHY

General works of methodology, specially adapted to ecclesiastical disciplines:

L. FONCK, *Wissenschaftliches Arbeiten*. Beiträge zur Methodik des akademischen Studiums. Innsbruck, Rauch, [3]1926. [A classical work which has inspired many other such works.]

ID., *Il metodo del lavoro scientifico*. Contributi alla pratica dello studio accademico. Roma, Pustet, 1909.

ID., *Le travail scientifique*. Ecole – Pratique. Paris, Beauchesne, 1911.

J. DE GUIBERT, *Breves Adnotiones in cursum Methodologiae Generalis*. Roma, P.U. Gregoriana, [2]1944.

Z. ALSZEGHY - M. FLICK, *Come si fa la Teologia*. Roma, Paoline, [3]1985.

ID., *Cómo se hace la teología*. Roma, Paolinas, 1976.

ID., *Introductory theology*. London, Sheed, 1982.

L. BOGLIOLO, *Guida alla ricerca scientifica e allo studio di S. Tommaso*. Roma, P.U. Lateranense, 1967.

J. DE GHELLINCK, *Les exercices pratiques du 'séminaire' en théologie*. Paris, Desclee de Brouwer, [4]1948.

G. YELLE, *Travail scientifique en disciplines ecclésiastiques*. Montréal, Grand Séminaire, 1945.

G. CARRIÈRE, *Précis de Méthodologie à l'usage des étudiants en Philosophie*. Ottawa, Univ., 1951.

I. GONSÁLEZ MORAL, *Metodologia*. Santander, Sal Terrae, [2]1960.

W. BEINERT, *Dogmatik studieren*. Einführung in dogmatisches Denken und Arbeiten. Regensburg, Pustet, 1985.

I. FRAGATA, *Noções de metodologia para a elaboração de um trabalho científico*. Porto, Tavares Martins, [2]1973.

On intellectual work:

A.D. SERTILLANGES, *La vie intellectuelle*. Son esprit, ses conditions, ses méthodes. Paris, Cerf, [53]1965.

ID., *La vita intellettuale*. Roma, Studium, 1945.

J. GUITTON, *Nouvel art de penser*. Paris, Aubier, 1951.

ID., *Arte nuova di pensare*. Milano, Paoline, [12]1988.

ID., *Le travail intellectuel*. Conseils a ceux qui étudient et a ceux qui écrivent. Paris, Aubier, 1951.

ID., *Il lavoro intellettuale*. Consigli a chi studia e lavora. Milano, Paoline, [12]1991.

W.M. BEVERIDGE, *The Art of Study. A guide to students*. London, Oxford University, 1965.

For technical details:

L. BOGLIOLO, *La tesi di laurea*. Guida al lavoro scientifico per gli studenti universitari. Torino, SEI, 1948.

U. ECO, *Come si fa una tesi di laurea*. Milano, Bompiani, 1985.

R. FARINA, *Metodologia. Avviamento alla tecnica del lavoro scientifico*. Rome, LAS, [4]1986.

A. FARINA – N. MARINONE, *Metodologia*. Guida pratica alle esercitazioni del seminario e alla tesi di laurea per le discipline umanistiche. Torino, SEI, 1979.

A. GALUZZI, *Appunti di metodologia*. Roma, P.U. Lateranense, [4]1983.

J. JANSSENS, *Note di metodologia*. Parte prima: Elenco bibliografico, Nota bibliografica, Stesura del testo. Rome, P.U. Gregoriana, 1988.

F. VAN STEENBERGHEN, *Directives pour la confection d'une monographie scientifique*. Avec applications concrètes aux recherches sur la philosophie médiévale. Louvain, Nauwelaerts, [3]1961.

E.S. BALIAN, *How to design, analyze and write doctoral research. The practical guidebook*. Lanham, Univ. Press of America, 1982.

R.A. DAY, *How to write and publish a scientific paper*. Philadelphia, ISI-Press, 1983.

S.A. MATCZAK, *Research and Composition in Philosophy*. Louvain-Paris, Nauwelaerts, 1968.

I. QUESADA HERRERA, *Redacción y presentación del trabajo intellectual*. Tesinas, Tesis doctorales, proyectos, memorias, monografías. Madrid, Paraninfo, [2]1987.

J.E. HEYDE, *Technik des wissenschaftlichen Arbeitens.* Berlin, Junker, [10]1970.

H. KLIEMANN, *Anleitungen zum wissenschaftlichen Arbeiten.* Eine Einführung in die Praxis. Freiburg, Rombach, [8]1973.

H. KLIEMANN, *So erarbeitet man Vorträge und Veröffentlichungen.* München, Heyne, 1984.

A. RAFFELT, *Proseminar Theologie.* Einführung in das wissenschaftliche Arbeiten und in die theologische Buchkunde. Freiburg, Herder, 1985.

F. STEGMÜLLER, *Ziele und Wege der Seminararbeit*, in: A. KOLPING, *Einführung in die katholische Theologie.* Münster, Regensberg, [2]1963, p. 187-201.

PART ONE

THE COURSE AND THE TEXTBOOK

1. The Course

1.1 *Course and textbook*

Aim. Courses and textbooks are meant to provide students, in the fastest and easiest way, with that *basic knowledge* of every subject without which they cannot proceed further in their studies.

Historical origin. The pair 'book' and 'course' takes its origin from the 'praelectio' of the medieval universities, where in the presence of his students the master used to 'read', i.e. comment upon, some authoritative text: Sacred Scripture, the 'Sentences' (extracts from the writings of the Fathers), Aristotle .... Gradually however, the systematic construction made by the master became more important, until the book taken as text became, in modern times, a simple complement (or even a substitute) to the 'lecture' of the master. Today, not even the normative texts of theology (Sacred Scripture, documents of the Magisterium) are commented upon passage by passage: even the very courses of exegesis are devoted to teaching the *methods* of interpretation.

Course and book - the difference. Sometimes it is said: "The advent of printed books has made the course superfluous." Is this true?

The *book* is *something* that can be handled. It can be rapidly glanced through; it can also be read slowly and repeatedly. The book is *something that lasts*. The same passage can be taken up many times and can be compared with

other passages of the same book. A book can contain and preserve *much information*. But the book *does not think* for me
and does not help me think, though it may stimulate my
thought.

In the *course*, a person is present. In his lecture, the professor *thinks* for me and with me. The lecture obliges the students to follow the pace of the professor. At the same time, it
helps them follow what is being said, because the development is articulated, the more important points are highlighted
(by means of the intonation, the gestures, the boardwork), the
difficult passages are repeated. The professor offers the information in such a way that it can be assimilated during the lecture itself, and he proposes it in a lively way so that at least
the essentials can be retained.

Complementarity of course and book. The course and
the text differ therefore with regard to the *manner* rather than
with regard to the *matter*. They are therefore complementary
in their didactical functions:

The course is the apt means when it is a question of
introducing the students to a *train of thought*, presenting
them a *panorama* of the current state of a discipline and
proposing them a sampling of its *method*.

The book is the suitable means when it is a question of
furnishing *supplementary information* and ensuring a *slow
assimilation*.

1.2 *How to follow a course*

In order to follow a course with greatest profit, one
must:

1.21 *Listen*. Follow the lecture of the professor with
attention. Do not let yourself be distracted by points which
remain obscure, or by your own 'meditations'. The obscure
points will probably be clarified as the lecture proceeds. Or
else, make a brief note (e.g. of unfamiliar words or names
that recur often) and clarify later. If your knowledge of the

language of the course is not very good, make sure you take a dictionary along with you.

1.22 *Dialogue*. The course is not like a reproduction from one tape to another. The student is not an blank tape or a 'tabula rasa'. Everyone has, and must have, his own preconceptions, problems and expectations. These enter (tacitly) into dialogue and sometimes into conflict with what the professor says. The course thus presents itself as a *response* (expected or unexpected) to the questions which every student carries within himself.

The more a course appears as a response, the more it "makes sense" and becomes intelligible. To benefit from a course one must therefore raise questions within oneself, expect something, *find out beforehand* what the course is dealing with (by looking up the text, examining the syllabus, revising the previous lecture), just as one finds out all the necessary information before going to the cinema!

This interior and tacit dialogue expresses itself in various gestures (often unconscious, but noticed by the professor) and sometimes through explicit *interventions* (asking for further explanation, raising difficulties, etc.) during the interval or even during the lecture. Such feedback helps the professor adapt his teaching to the students.

1.23 *Follow*. What should interest me in a course is not the ideas which it evokes in me, nor the confirmation of what I already know, but the *new things* which I can learn. I must therefore concentrate attention and the effort to understand on what is new (and sometimes unexpected) in the lecture. Therefore it is useful *to pay attention to:* new words or names which recur often (or which the professor stresses), and in general to all that is highlighted or repeated several times or written on the board (if I find nothing new, probably I have not understood the lecture properly); to the criticisms of other opinions (the contrast makes it easier to understand what is being said); to the examples (without losing sight of what these are meant to illustrate).

In this way, the student "follows" the professor along new paths, letting go and leaving behind what he already knows and thinks.

1.24 *Write.* In order to conserve the fruits of such attention and to return to it later (deepening, clarifying ...), it is absolutely necessary to *take down some notes* during the lecture. Here we can distinguish two cases:

1.241 *If there is a text* or notes which the course follows quite faithfully, it is normally enough to make some notes *on the book itself:* underlining (in different colors perhaps), making signs in the margin (cf. 2.22 below), noting additional points briefly. To take notes of more substantial additions or comments made by the professor, papers may be inserted into the book itself (making sure to note on every paper the page and paragraph referred to!).

1.242 *If there is no text*, more complete notes must be taken, which reproduce (while abbreviating and simplifying) the development of the lecture. Such notes are taken on *large-size* papers (or better on notebooks), so that one can write in such a way that the points can be taken in at a glance, and so that further additions can be inserted later. (For the same reason one should not normally write in shorthand, unless one reads it perfectly; one could instead make use of a system of abbreviations). *One must take note most especially* of all the *divisions* into which the professor divides the subject matter (these will be naturally also the divisions of the notes), of the *material information* which he gives (bibliography, sources, names, etc.) as well as of his *explanations* (but of these one must note only the essential, in such a way as to be able later to reconstruct the discourse of the professor; e.g. by noting the examples with some catchword). The digressions which the professor sometimes makes may possibly be noted down (if they are interesting), but must be indicated as such (by including the whole passage within parentheses (...)). The same holds for one's own ideas which arise during a lecture: these must always be included within square brackets [...].

The art of taking notes is not learnt within a day. Normally there is a tendency to write too much. The ideal would be to write no more than what is necessary to reconstruct the essentials of the lecture. This presupposes that one writes in an intelligent way, *understanding* what is being said. Forcing oneself to take good notes is therefore a wonderful way of *actively* following a course (or a conference ...).

NB 1: Should one take down all that is on the board? Not necessarily; sometimes the board serves only to stress what is being said. *Names* however are written so as to be copied down; it is also very useful to take down the *schemes* which may be given.

NB 2: Is it useful to *tape a discourse?* Unless one does it for the benefit of others (and then one must have the explicit permission of the professor!), *it is difficult to see the usefulness* of this. The re-hearing of the tape would take as much time as the lecture itself, and it is not the particular words of the professor that are important. It would be more useful to spend this time going through the notes taken (which are far more brief) and deepening them (cf. 5.2 - 5.4 below).

PRACTICAL EXERCISES:

1. Having read the indications given in the "Programme of studies", say what you expect from each course.

2. Compare and discuss the notes taken from one or several lectures, whether they are clear, sufficient, superfluous.

2. The Textbook

2.1 *'Manuals' and 'Notes'*

Two types of textbooks can be distinguished.

Manuals (usually written by someone else, not by the one giving the course) present the matter *in a systematic manner*, independently of the course, and therefore supply plenty of *supplementary information* (while the course will try to bring the manual *up to date,* wherever necessary).

Notes, prepared by the professor who is giving the course (be careful of the notes prepared by the students themselves: they often contain big mistakes!) are only *an aid for following the course more easily* (practically relieving one of the necessity of taking notes).

Both types of textbooks are merely *aids* to help follow and eventually fill in the course, and to prepare better for the examinations.

They are not sufficient by themselves, neither for the examinations nor as a basis for further studies. There is need of the course and of further reading.

By way of information, here are a *series of manuals*, which can be consulted for the systematic disciplines in philosophy and theology:

2.11 *For systematic philosophy:*

Institutiones Philosophiae Scholasticae. Auctoribus pluribus philosophiae professoribus in Collegio Pullacensi Societatis Jesu. 7 vol. Freiburg, etc., Herder, 1949-59. [One of the last and, all said and done, one of the better series of philosophical texts in Latin.]

S. VANNI ROVIGHI, *Elementi di filosofia.* 3 vol. Brescia, La Scuola, ³1962-64. [Brief, but useful for a first consultation.]

Cours de Philosophie Thomiste. 7 vol. Paris, Beauchesne, ²1959-64. [Produced by the professors of the Institut Catholique de Paris; short, substantial; these 7 volumes are accompanied by 8 others of history and of texts.]

ID., *Corso di filosofia tomista.* 7 vol. Brescia, Paideia, 1966-67.

ID., *Curso de filosofía tomista.* 7 vol. Barcelona, Herder, 1968-69.
F. GABORIAU, *Nouvelle initiation philosophique.* 5 vol. Paris, Casterman, 1962-65.
R. JOLIVET, *Traité de Philosophie.* 4 vol. Lyon-Paris, Vitte. [8]1963-66.
ID., *Trattato di Filosofia.* 7 vol. Brescia, Morcelliana, 1957-60.
Grundkurs Philosophie (Urban Taschenbücher). Stuttgart, Kohlhammer, 1982-86 [Produced by the professors of the Jesuit Faculty of Philosophy at Munich; to the 5 volumes of systematic philosophy must be added the 5 other volumes of the history of philosophy].
ID., *Corso fundamental de filosofía.* Barcelona, Herder, 1986-87.

2.12 *For systematic theology* the more recent series (reflecting the theology of the Council) are, for the most part, still *incomplete:*

C. ROCCHETTA, *Corso di teologia sistematica.* 8 vol. to date. Bologna, Dehoniane, 1985-
Le mystère chrétien. Théologie dogmatique. 9 volumes to date.
Théologie sacramentaire. 3 volumes to date.
Théologie morale. 3 volumes to date.
Tournai, Desclée, 1962- [Brief and substantial; publication has been suspended].
ID., *Il mistero cristiano.* Teologia dogmatica. 4 vol. to date.
Teologia sacramentaria. 2 vol. to date.
Roma, Desclée, 1966-
ID., *El misterio cristiano.* 16 volumes to date. Barcelona, Herder, 1968.
J. DORÉ (ed.), *Le christianisme et la foi chrétienne.* Manuel de théologie. 4 volumes to date. Paris, Declée, 1985-
B. LAURET – F. REFOULÉ (ed.), *Initiation à la pratique de la théologie.* 5 vol. Paris, Cerf, 1982-83.
ID., *Iniziazione alla pratica della teologia.* 5 vol. Brescia, Queriniana, 1986-87.
ID., *Iniciación a la prática de la teología.* 4 volumes to date. Madrid, Cristianidad, 1984-85.
ID., *Neue Summe Theologie* (ed. P. EICHER) 3 vol. Freiburg, Herder, 1988-89.
J.H. NICOLAS, *Synthèse dogmatique. De la Trinité à la Trinité.* Paris: Beauchesne, 1985.

Historia salutis. Seria de monografías de Teología dogmatica. 12 volumes to date. Madrid, BAC, 1968- (vol. 282, 292, 294, 316, 322, 388-339, 346, 360, 392, 412, 482).
Some of these volumes have been translated into Italian in the series: *Testi di teologia.* Roma, Paoline, 1970-
CELAM, *Teología para la Evangelización liberadora en América Latina.* Colección de textos básicos para seminaries latinoamericanos. 5 volumes to date. Bogotá, CELAM, 1984-
ID., *Grande corso di Teologia Fondamentale e Dogmatica.* 4 volumes to date. Casale Monferrato, Piemme, 1988-
Mysterium salutis. Grundriss heilsgeschichtlicher Dogmatik. 6 vol. Einsiedeln, Benziger, 1965-76. [The manual most referred to today, but rather too extensive and too 'speculative' for a first consultation.]

Complemented by:
M. LÖHRER – Chr. SCHÜTZ – D. WIEDERKEHR (ed.), *Arbeitshilfen und Weiterführung.* Einsiedeln, Benziger, 1981.
ID., *Mysterium salutis.* Nuovo corso di dogmatica come teologia della storia della salvezza. 12 vol. Brescia, Queriniana, 1967-78.
ID., *Mysterium salutis.* Manuál de teología como historia de la salvación. 8 volumes to date. Madrid, Cristianidad, 1969-
ID., *Mysterium salutis.* Dogmatique de l'histoire du salut. 14 volumes to date. Paris, Cerf, 1969-
J. AUER – J. RATZINGER, *Kleine katholische Dogmatik.* 9 vol. Regensburg, Pustet, 1970-83.
ID., *Piccola dogmatica cattolica.* 6 volumes to date. Assisi, Citadella, 1971-
ID., *Curso de teología dogmática.* 9 vol. Barcelona, Herder, 1975-91.
M. SCHMAUS, *Der Glaube der Kirche. Handbuch einer katholischen Dogmatik.* 2 vol. München, Hueber, 1969-70.
ID., *Der Glaube der Kirche.* 14 vol. St. Ottilien, EOS, [2]1979-82 [the only recent manual written by a single author].
ID., *Dogmatica cattolica.* Ed. N. BUSSI. 6 vol. Torino, Marietti, [2]1974-75.
S. PIÉ I NINOT, *Tratado de Teología Fundamental.* Salamanca, Secretariado Trinitario, 1989.
W. KERN, alii. *Handbuch der Fundamentaltheologie.* 4 vol. Freiburg, Herder, 1985-88.

ID., *Corso di teologia fundamentale.* Brescia, Queriniana, 1990.

Finally, we indicate a collection of simple texts which cover the whole range of seminary studies:

Manuale di base Piemme. 37 vols. Casale Monferrato, Piemme, 1991-

2.13 To the manuals of systematic theology, one may add today the *specialized encyclopedias* of the various disciplines:

R. LATOURELLE – R. FISICHELLA, *Dizionario di teologia fondamentale.* Assisi, Cittadella, 1990.

G. RUGGIERI, *Enciclopedia di teologia fondamentale.* Storia, Progetto, Autori, Categorie. 1 volume to date. Casale Monferrato, Marietti, 1987-

M. O'CARROLL, *Trinitas.* A Theological Encyclopedia of the Holy Trinity. Wilmington DE, Glazier, 1987.

ID., *Corpus Christi.* An Encyclopedia of the Eucharist. Wilmington DE, Glazier, 1988.

ID., *Theotokos.* A Theological Encyclopedia of the Blessed Virgin. Wilmington DE, Glazier, 1983.

S. DE FIORES – S. MEO, *Nuovo dizionario di mariologia.* Milano, Paoline, 1985.

R. BÄUMER – L. SCHEFFZYK, *Marienlexikon.* 3 volumes to date. St. Ottilien, EOS, 1988-

F. ROBERTI – P. PALAZZINI, *Dizionario di teologia morale.* 2 vol. Roma, Studium, [4]1968.

ID., *Dictionary of Moral Theology.* Westminster, MD, Newman, 1962.

L. ROSSI – A. VALSECCHI, *Dizionario enciclopedico di teologia morale.* Roma, Paoline, [6]1985.

ID., *Diccionario enciclopédico de teología moral.* Madrid, Paulinas, 1974.

F. COMPAGNONI – G. PIANA – S. PRIVITERA, *Nuovo Dizionario di Teologia morale.* Torino, Paoline, 1990. [Replaces Rossi-Valsecchi.]

I. MACQUARRIE – J. CHILDRESS, *A New Dictionary of Christian Ethics.* London, SCM Press, 1986.

O. HÖFFE, *Lexicon der Ethik*. München, Beck, [3]1986.
ID., *Dictionnaire de Morale*. Fribourg, Éd. Universitaires, 1983.
K. HÖRMANN, *Lexikon der christlichen Moral*. Innsbruck, Tyrolia, [2]1976.
ID., *Diccionario de moral cristiana*. Barcelona, Herder, 1975.
B. STOECKLE, *Wörterbuch christlicher Ethik*. (Herderbücherei, 533). Freiburg, Herder, [2]1980.
ID., *Dizionario di etica cristiana*. Assisi, Cittadella, 1978.

2.2 *How to use the textbook*

The textbook must be used according to the indications of the professor. In order to draw the maximum profit one must:

2.21 *Understand the book*. This is not a question of learning the book by heart! The textbook can and must be 'understood': it must be grasped in its totality, in such a way that the parts are illumined by their position in the whole and by the relations among themselves. To understand a book, one first *looks at it as a whole*, meditating (not merely glancing) at the *Table of Contents* (which gives the structure and the development of the book); then one reads the *Preface* and/or the *Introduction* (where the author indicates the scope and the limits of the book and/or the problems discussed, often giving a brief summary of what he intends to say).

In order to understand the individual parts, one must not only always keep in mind the overall structure, but also refer frequently to other parts of the book, making *comparisons*. For this, the *Analytical Indices* (of names and/or of concepts) are useful.

2.22 *Take notes,* or leave the traces of such an active reading (preferably in pencil, so that one can erase them if necessary) — naturally *only in books belonging to oneself,* never in those belonging to the library! The following signs may be used in the margin:

? = I have not understood this point (after trying repeatedly)

	= important passage or formulation, to be remembered
→	= the key point of the problem (or an expression of the author which clarifies everything; or an assertion which I must still discuss at length)
!	= something which I would not have expected at this point; why this? A point to be kept in mind!
↔ p.28	= seems to be in contradiction with what is said on p. 28 (at least at first sight)
Cfr.p.28	= connect with what is on p.28; compare! (similarly: cf. Gilbert, cf. the platonic ideas = connect with what is said in the course of prof. Gilbert, or with what I know about the platonic ideas, etc.).

(NB: here also one can put in square brackets [...] what one wants to characterize as subjective notes, e.g. [?] = this seems doubtful *to me* (but maybe it is not).

Besides one can use *highlighters* (or underline in different colors) to mark not entire passages (otherwise the highlighting becomes insignificant), but *words* and *important formulations;* using the colors in such a way as to aid the visual memory (e.g. pink for new concepts and definitions; yellow for names of philosophers or theologians; green for important places of Sacred Scripture or for the central ideas of a philosophical argument, etc.).

2.23 *Consult it again and again.* Normally the textbook contains far more information than is immediately necessary, especially as far as *bibliographical indications* are concerned. One must know how to use these wisely even later on (cf. 7.13, 7.4 below), before searching for further bibliography.

Besides, it may be useful to *re-read*, at some later stage of one's studies, some chapter of the initial textbooks, when one comes across a problem or a concept already discussed before, so as to bring it into sharp focus. One will realize that now one understands much better and more deeply what the textbook was saying.

To orientate oneself in such a re-consultation, one can make use of the Analytical Index, if there is one.

NB: The older philosophical texts use the scholastic form of the 'theses'. The 'thesis' is a *brief and condensed formulation*, in a single proposition, of the solution which the master intends giving to a particular problem. Having thus indicated the conclusion of the discourse, a more detailed exposition is given.

After having briefly *situated the problem* ('Sensus thesis', 'Aim', 'Nexus'), the *new notions* ('Terms', 'Praenotiones', 'Explanations') necessary for understanding and resolving the problem are explained; then *other solutions* ('Opinions', 'Sententia') to the same problem are presented; finally the reasons for the solution adopted are given ('Probatur thesis', 'Proofs').

To this there are sometimes added *further consequences* which follow from what has been affirmed in the thesis ('Corollary'), responses to *possible difficulties* ('Objections') and *other considerations* more or less connected with the thesis ('Scholion').

The thesis form of exposition has the merit of being clear and therefore easily assimilable; today however the 'genetic' mode of exposition is usually preferred, which allows the student to follow the progressive genesis of problems and, consequently, of their solutions.

Inversely, the rigid and clear structure of the 'Thesis' can be a very good guide for (clarifying and) exposing one's opinion. From a scheme made in the form of a 'Thesis' one can easily draw out a good conference or article.

PRACTICAL EXERCISES:

1. Analyze in common the Table of Contents of various textbooks and compare them.

2. Compare the textbook of a course with the lectures already given: What does the book add to the lectures? What did these add to the book? Do this for various courses and make a comparison.

3. For books which are not in the mother-tongue of the students: Translate some passage of the book into one's own language; compare the translations made by different students.

PART TWO

GROUP WORK

3. Groups

The course and the textbook provide only the matter of knowledge. In order to make of this his *own* personal knowledge, the student must assimilate it and deepen it through *personal study*. He must therefore reserve a definite amount of time *every day* for such study, so as not to fall too far behind what is being taught.

A good part of personal study may be done *better* and *more effectively* in small study groups and/or in coordination with such groups. Such group work has the following advantages: *dividing* the work among the members of the group, the *gains are increased*, in so far as each one profits by the work of the others; the *sharing of ideas* (and also of unresolved problems) and of the fruits of research brings with it an *enrichment* and an enlargement of each one's horizon of knowing; in the *discussion* of problems and discoveries, there is mutual *control* over the quality of work done by each one. When there are groups that work well, the professor can entrust to them a good part of the work of assimilation of the basic material, reserving the lectures for more specialized explanations.

A group consists of *two to six members*; if the number is greater, there will inevitably be some 'passive' members. The groups may be *stable* or may be set up for particular tasks. The *stable groups* are far more efficient and fruitful, if not for any other reason, at least because the members are *familiar* with the habits of work and of discussion of each one. In the course of the first cycle, every student should participate in some stable group (but not necessarily always in the same group).

A stable study group can and should undertake *two types of work:*

3.1 *Private work subsequently put in common*

A good part of the assimilative study consists in assignments, such as filling in historical information (cf. 5.3), information regarding terminology (5.1 and 5.41 below), the finding out of parallels in Sacred Scripture (5.212 below), which must be done *individually*, but which need *not necessarily* be done entirely *by every student*. In such cases, the work may be *divided* among the members of a group, and the results may subsequently be *put together*.

The *division of work* is done in the first meeting of the group. The group establishes what information is to be sought, and assigns each member a part of this research. In a second meeting, the individuals *communicate the results* of their research, in a concise and clear way, so that *all can take note*. The brief (!) questions for clarification and the answers help to check and to make the results more precise, and to determine whether there is any further research to be done.

It is useful that every now and then the tasks be divided in a different way, so that each one may have the opportunity and the obligation to familiarize himself with all the different types of research.

NB: *The drawing up of summaries should never be divided in this way* (5.5 below), because the value of these lies not so much in the result (often of little significance except for the one who has written the summary) as in the work of elaboration. However, these may be *edited in common*.

The re-elaboration of *class notes* may instead be assigned to a member of the group, *provided that* all those who use the notes have *attended* the course in question, taking some personal notes. Otherwise, instead of the explanations of the professor, they will receive only what some other student has understood (or misunderstood). **In brief: notes made by others can never substitute attendance at lectures.**

3.2 *Discussion and elaboration in common*

When it is a question not so much of gathering information as of *understanding* more deeply, the group will work in common, *discussing* both what each one thinks he has understood and above all *the points that remain obscure*, as well as the *difficulties* that arise against the teaching proposed by the professor or presented by the textbook.

Such discussion is *indispensable* for the study of speculative subjects, such as systematic philosophy and theology. "Discussion is essential for philosophy. What does it mean to philosophize? It means to give an account of, to search the reasons of things, to affirm only after having reflected and on the basis of evidence. To discuss means that two or more persons check or examine something. Discussion provides one of the best means for affirming something after having discussed it and on the basis of evidence ..." (M. BLONDEL, *Carnets Intimes* II, p. 205). Besides this, discussion obliges one to *express oneself clearly*, and the sharing of ideas and of difficulties brings new light, because one will have understood a certain point better, while someone else some other point or aspect.

3.21 *The rules to be observed in a good discussion* regard above all the basic attitudes. It is necessary to have:
— *Discipline:* keep to the theme and *speak to the point;* speak *briefly* (and only when you really have something to say); make an effort to express yourself *clearly* (indicating the point being made, distinguishing and organizing your ideas, not bringing in too many ideas in a single intervention).
— *Receptivity:* know how to *listen* (without trying to think out your own ideas at the same time), make an effort to understand the intervention of the other *from his point of view* (not

getting lost in details, but evaluating what has been said in its totality and in the context of the whole discussion), *checking your own understanding through some question for clarification*, or by repeating briefly what has been said, being ready to *accept* even ideas and opinions for which you have little 'sympathy'.

— *Sincerity:* do not try to make your own opinion prevail, nor champion its cause, but *search the truth together.* For this, be ready to reveal to the others even your own presuppositions and 'prejudices' and doubts.

— *Courage: dare to say* what you think (or what you fail to understand) without conformistic reticence (accommodation to 'public opinion'); nor should you be afraid *to reveal your personality.*

— *Order:* allow everyone *equal opportunities to speak*; do not let the discussion be side-tracked onto marginal subjects; *situate* your interventions in the total context, taking note of what has been said before. In order to assure such order, whenever the membership of the group exceeds three or four persons, *there is always need of a coordinator*; this person, through discreet interventions, will make sure that everyone has a say and that the discussion does not deviate.

3.22 In order to reactivate a discussion that seems 'grounded', the method of 'brainstorming' may be useful: each one says, without any particular order, whatever comes to mind regarding the theme under discussion; *there is no criticism* or discussion of what is said, but after some time it becomes possible to reactivate the discussion on the basis of the material thus collected.

NB: Provided these rules are observed, it may be very fruitful to have a *collaboration between students of different capacities* (those who are smart and quick to grasp, and those who are weak and slow) and/or different interests in the same study group. Both parties will derive profit.

3.3 *Other forms of work in groups*

Other ways of working in groups that are more organized and guided, and which are normally formed for particular tasks, are described in: Z. ALSZEGHY - M. FLICK, *Come si fa la Teologia*, p. 183-187.

PRACTICAL EXERCISE: Make a self-criticism of the work done in group in the proseminar. Identify the causes of what did not go well, and ask yourself how to remedy the situation. (A brainstorming would be a very good idea ...).

4. The Seminar

Stable study groups are mostly spontaneous, restricted, and without a fixed program of work. A seminar instead, which should have even more *stability* (it should last at least a whole semester), is conducted under the *direction of a professor* (or assistant), has a *fixed program of work,* concentrates on *a single theme,* and may take in *a larger number of participants* (up to 15 or 20). Study groups are concerned mainly with assimilative study (5 below); while the seminar helps *to initiate the student to scientific research* (7-10 below).

'Seminars' originated in the departments of History and Philology in the German Universities of the 19th century, and were meant originally as initiations into the *methods of research and criticism in philology and history* and consequently also in philosophy and theology. As such they constitute an essential and indispensable part of every university formation in these areas.

The practical initiation which seminars give is naturally *progressive.* Before being able to collaborate in a real seminar, it is necessary to have a *first initiation* to methods of work in a *proseminar.* This may be either a course of *methodology with written exercises* (as in the case of the present book), or a *seminar with a more modest theme,* from which new scientific results are not expected, but which insists instead on the methodological aspect. In this sense, the seminars of the first cycles of Philosophy and Theology would all actually be proseminars.

When, in the higher cycles, study is oriented more and more towards personal research, *the seminars also slowly become more important than the courses*.

4.1 *How a seminar is conducted*

A seminar is characterized by its *regularity* (weekly or fortnightly meetings over at least one semester); by the *guidance of a professor* (or assistant), who proposes the theme and plans at least the preliminary division of work; by a *single thematic* and above all by the *active collaboration* required of the students.

The theme of a seminar can be either the *analytic interpretation* of a work (or of a scriptural or doctrinal text) or the *elaboration of a synthesis*, gathering and putting together all that has been written about a specific problem. For the early seminars, the interpretation of a text seems to give results that are more satisfying, because the success of the seminar depends on the *convergence of the work* of the individual participants: each one must be in a position to discuss with competence what is proposed by the other. This becomes easier when all have read the same work.

In the meetings of the seminar it is not the professor who speaks and proposes. He will have given a brief exposition of the theme at the beginning, with bibliographical indications, and he will have distributed the themes to be treated. Then, in every meeting, one or two *students present the results* of their research (e.g. the interpretation of a chapter) and *submit them to discussion* by the group. Sometimes the discussion is initiated by a 'respondent' who has the task of evaluating critically what has been said by the speaker. The *professor* intervenes only as a 'technical consultant' to help and encourage the discussion, and only at the end does he conclude by summarizing the results and by giving some critical judgment of his own.

The results of these expositions/debates are *preserved* in three ways: the speakers hand out to all a *brief written scheme* of their reports (which helps the others to follow the reports more easily). They later put down their reports in writing *taking into account the results of the discussion.* Besides this, it is very useful to have someone take the *minutes* of the discussions of each meeting, which will be read at the beginning of the next discussion (thus assuring continuity in the discussions). The 'dossier' of a well-conducted seminar (written reports and minutes) can become material for a book or a scientific article.

4.2 *How to collaborate in a seminar*

Participation in a seminar always calls for *active collaboration*, one that is so *intense* that it is normally impossible to register oneself simultaneously for two seminars.

It is fundamental that *all the participants be present at every meeting.* Those who for some grave reason cannot be present must *inform* the director of the seminar *before the meeting* takes place.

When the themes are distributed, each one must choose a theme proportionate to his capacities and possibilities, and must *immediately begin to prepare his own report* (as will be explained, cf. below 8.1), because only thus will he enter into the general thematic of the seminar. Some initial reading to orientate oneself may also be useful.

Each one must *prepare himself* at least broadly *for each meeting*, reading the chapter which is to be interpreted or familiarizing himself with the theme or author going to be exposed. During the *discussions*, each one must contribute whatever there is to say from the point of view which he has been assigned, and must take note of whatever may be useful in the treatment of the theme assigned to him.

The report must be prepared carefully; but at the meeting, rather than reading out from the text (this is difficult to follow), it would be better to present it in a form that is somewhat freer but nonetheless *concise.* A *brief written scheme* distributed to all the participants helps them follow the oral report more easily (especially when there are difficulties of language), and enables them to orient themselves in the discussion that follows.

The definitive draft of the report (which is handed over by each one in a written form) is made only *towards the end of the seminar*, so as to be able to take into account all that has been clarified by other reports and by the discussions. Only in this way will the written reports really bring together the fruits of the work of the group.

PART THREE

STUDY FOR ASSIMILATION

Up to now we have considered the *'institutional'* means for the acquisition of new knowledge (courses, manuals, study groups, seminars), and we have spoken of a collaboration which is still largely receptive. But in order to really assimilate and *appropriate* the knowledge offered, there is needed a *more personal effort* which each one must undertake for himself. *Assimilative study*, which will be considered in this third part and which is still concerned principally with *what is proposed in the courses*, will transform itself slowly into *creative study*, where it is the *student himself and his interests* which will determine the choice of readings and the themes to be developed in the various written works.

5. Personal Study

After having overcome the initial *difficulties of terminology* (5.1 Noting the terminology), in private study one must enter into repeated and prolonged contact with the primary or secondary *sources* (5.2 Access to the sources; 5.3 Completing the historical information), with the intention of *appropriating the new knowledge in a personal way* (5.4 Rethinking the doctrine), so as to be able to *express it in one's own words* (5.5 Writing a summary). As we have already said (3.1), a good part of this personal study can be done more profitably in study groups.

5.1 *Noting the terminology*

The initial feeling of dismay which one often has when

beginning the study of a new science, arises in large measure because of the *terminology* itself which is completely novel and which the professor and the manuals use glibly as if it were already familiar to the student. In fact, because our knowledge is composed of experiences and of 'notions', or of meaningful words, studying a science means, in large measure, *learning a new language*. This is particularly true for philosophy and theology, which aim not so much at introducing one to new fields of experience, as at teaching one *to reason and speak with methodical and critical rigor* of that which every man and every believing christian in fact 'already knows'.

The first task of personal study will therefore be to *arrive at an understanding* of the new terminology, in such a way that one will be able to *use it fluently and correctly*. It is therefore necessary:

5.11 *To search in a dictionary* the *meanings of words* which are unknown or whose exact meaning is not clear, and which *recur often* in the courses and textbooks. Besides the dictionaries in one's own language, for such a preliminary consultation there are different *small specialized dictionaries*.

For philosophy:

A BIRAGHI, *Dizionario di Filosofia*. Milano, Comunità, 1957 [On pp. 631-667: Breve dizionario dei termini greci e tedeschi].
P.E. LAMANNA – F. ADORNO. *Dizionario dei termini filosofici*. Firenze, Le Monnier, [17]1969.
E. MORSELLI, *Dizionario di filosofia e scienze umane*. Milano, Signorelli, [2]1988.
J. DIDIER, *Dictionnaire de la philosophie*. Paris, Larousse, 1973.
P. FOULQUIÉ – R. SAINT-JEAN. *Dictionnaire de la langue philosophique*. Paris, PUF, [2]1969.
R. JOLIVET, *Vocabulaire de la philosophie*, suivi d'un tableau historique des écoles de philosophie. Lyon, Vitte, [6]1966.
ID., *Dizionario di filosofia*, con un prospetto storico delle scuole di filosofia. Brescia, Morcelliana, 1966.

A. FLEW, *Dictionary of Philosophy.* London, Macmillan, 1979.

A.R. LACEY, *A Dictionary of Philosophy.* London, Routledge, 1976.

D.D. RUNES, *The Dictionary of Philosophy.* New York, Philosophical Library, [2]1942.

ID., *Dizionario di filosofia.* 2 vol. Segrate, Mondadori, [6]1982.

B. WUELLNER, *Dictionary of Scholastic Philosophy.* Milwaukee, Bruce, 1956.

J. FERRATER MORA, *Diccionario de filosfía abreviada.* Barcelona, Edhasa, 1976.

J. ZARAGÜETA, *Vocabulario filosófico.* Madrid, Espasa, 1955.

W. BRUGGER, *Philosophisches Wörterbuch.* Freiburg, Herder, [3]1987.

ID., *Dizionario di Filosofia.* Torino, Marietti, 1959.

ID., *Philosophical Dictionary.* Ed. K. BAKER. Spokane, Gonzaga Univ., 1972.

ID., *Diccionario de Filosofia.* Barcelona, Herder, [8]1975.

M. MÜLLER – A. HALDER, *Philosophisches Wörterbuch* (Herder Tb. 1579). Freiburg, Herder, [2]1990.

F. RICKEN, *Lexikon der Erkenntnistheorie und Metaphysik.* München, Beck, 1984.

For scholastic terminology in Latin:

N. SIGNORIELLO, *Lexicon peripateticum philosophico-theologicum.* Roma, Pustet, [5]1931.

M.F. GARCIA, *Lexicon scholasticum philosophico-theologicum.* Reprint, Hildesheim, Olms, 1974. [For Scotist terminology].

L. SCHÜTZ, *Thomas-Lexikon.* Paderborn, Schöningh, [2]1895. Reprint, Stuttgart, Frommann, [2]1983.

R.I. DEFERRARI, alii, *A Lexicon of St. Thomas Aquinas on the Summa Theologica and other selected pages of his works.* Washington, Catholic Univ., 1948-54.

For theology:

G. BARBAGLI – S. DIANICH, *Nuovo dizionario di teologia.* 1 vol. + Supplemento I. Roma, Paoline, [5]1988.

ID., *Nuevo Diccionario de Teología.* 2 vol. Madrid, Cristianidad, 1982.

G. CANOBBIO, *Piccolo lessico di teologia*. Brescia, Morcelliana, 1989.

U. PROCII, *Breve dizionario dei termini e dei concetti biblici più usati*. Torino, ElleDiCi, 1988.

L. BOUYER, *Dictionnaire théologique*. Paris, Desclée, [2]1963.

ID., *Diccionario de teología*. Barcelona, Herder, [4]1977.

Y. CONGAR – G. SIEGWALT, *Vocabulaire oecuménique*. Paris, Cerf, 1970.

ID., *Dizionario ecumenico*. Assisi, Cittadella, 1982.

V.A. HARVEY, *Handbook of Theological Terms*. London, Bagster, 1977 [protestant].

J.A. KOMONCHAK, M. COLLINS, D.A. LANE (ed.), *The New Dictionary of Theology*. Wilmington DE, Glazier, 1987.

A.J. NEWIS, *The Maryknoll Catholic Dictionary*. New York, Grosset, 1965.

G. FLUR SERRANO – L. ALONSO SCHÖCKEL, *Diccionario terminológico de la ciencia bíblica*. Valencia, Institución San Jerónimo, 1979. [Extremely useful, contains also translations of technical terms in German, English and Italian, besides a bibliography].

ID., *Dizionario terminologico della scienza biblica*. Roma, Borla, 1981.

ID., *Petit vocabulaire des etudes bibliques*. Paris, Cerf, 1982.

K. RAHNER – H. VORGRIMLER, *Kleines theologisches Wörterbuch*. (Herderbücherei 557). Freiburg, Herder [16]1988.

ID., *Dizionario di teologia*. Brescia, Morcelliana, 1968.

ID., *Petit dictionnaire de théologie catholique*. Paris, Seuil, 1968.

ID., *Dictionary of Theology*. New York, Crossroads, [2]1990.

W. BRÄNDLE, *Taschenbuch theologischer Fremdwörter*. Gütersloh, Mohn, 1982. [Very brief].

F. HAUCK – G. SCHWINGE, *Theologisches Fach- und Fremdwörterbuch*. Göttingen, Vandenhoeck, [6]1987.

One should always have at hand one of these little dictionaries whenever one is studying anything.

5.12 *Check the usage* of the new terminology: *the context in which* the professor (and better still, the professors) and the textbook use it, the *examples* they give, the *distinctions* they

introduce (because the meaning of a word is made more precise by indicating that which it does *not* mean). On the basis of
this 'linguistic experience', try to *distinguish* the new term
from its (quasi-)synonyms, find appropriate *examples*, and
finally *translate* it into your own language (if this is different
from the medium of instruction) or at any rate into *everyday
language.* (The pastoral importance of this last exercise is evident.)

PRACTICAL EXERCISES: 1. Look up the same
unknown term in different dictionaries. Do the explanations
agree? Discuss the divergences that emerge.
2. Check the use of a new term in the way described
(5.12); write down the distinction between synonyms, one or
two examples, the translation, and discuss these.

5.2 *For theology: Going to the sources*

As a science, theology bases itself completely upon and
receives its norms from the *sources of revelation*: Sacred
Scripture and Tradition, authentically interpreted by the
Magisterium of the church. The principal task of personal
study in theology will therefore be a constant and direct contact with these sources, with the aim of becoming familiar with
them. What the course and/or the textbook can indicate merely briefly, should be repeatedly read and 'ruminated' upon in
the sources themselves.

5.21 *Reading Sacred Scripture:* Sacred Scripture is the soul
of theology. A good part of the courses (Introduction, Exegesis)
are meant to teach the student how to read Sacred Scripture correctly. It is the task of personal study *to make the connection*
between this scriptural teaching, and what is taught in dogmatics
and in moral theology. Besides a rapid reading of the *whole* of
Sacred Scripture (beginning from the New Testament), which
must be done during the first years of study, one must *re-read,
within the context* and possibly in the original, (for the New

Testament) *all* the Scriptural texts referred to in the systematic courses. Rather than trying to throw more light on these texts by means of a *commentary* (except when the text is particularly obscure), it is more useful to *turn to the parallel texts*.

Aids:

5.211 For the *Greek text* of the New Testament, the most accessible and handy edition is that of K. ALAND and others (Stuttgart, Deutsche Bibelstiftung, [26]1979; the English edition, United Bible Societies, [3]1975, is supplemented with a Greek-English Dictionary). This can be compared to the Latin text: A. MERK (Roma, P.I. Biblico, [9]1969) and E. NESTLE – K. ALAND (Stuttgart, Württembergische Bibelanstalt, [22]1963).

Aids for a reading of the Greek text:

M. ZERWICK, *Analysis philologica Novi Testamenti graeci*. Roma, P.I. Biblico, [3]1966.

ID., - M. GROSVENOR, *A Grammatical Analysis of the Greek New Testament*. Roma, P.I. Biblico, 1984.

FR. ZORELL, *Lexicon graecum Novi Testamenti*. Roma, P.I. Biblico, [3]1978.

C. BUZZETTI, *Dizionario base del Nuovo Testamento greco-italiano*. Roma, Libreria Sacre Scritture, 1989.

S. KUBO, *A Reader's Greek-English Lexicon of the New Testament*. Leiden, Brill, [4]1973.

I.P. LOUW – F.A. NIDA, *Greek-English Lexicon of the New Testament*, based on Semantic Domains. 2 vol. New York, United Bible Soceieties, 1988-89. [Ordered according to topics, with an alphabetical index in the second volume].

Complete Categorised Greek-English New Testament Vocabulary. London, Bagster, 1978.

M. GUERRA, *Diccionario morfológico del Nuevo Testamento*. Burgos, Aldecora, 1978.

M. CARREZ – F. MOREL, *Dictionnaire grec-français du Nouveau Testament*. Neuchâtel, Delachaux, 1972.

W. BAUER – K. ALAND, *Griechisch-Deutsches Wörterbuch zu den*

Schriften des Neuen Testaments und der frühchristlichen Literatur. Berlin, Gruyter, [6]1988.
ID., *A Greek-English Lexicon of the New Testament and other Early Christian Literature*. Ed. W.F. ARNDT – F.W. GINGRICH. Chicago-Cambridge, Univ. Press, [3]1963.
E. PREUSCHEN, *Griechisch-deutsches Taschenwörterbuch zum Neuen Testament*. Berlin, Gruyter, [6]1976.

5.212 For *comparing* parallel texts, one will find plenty of material in the marginal notes of the editions of MERK and of NESTLE, and also in the margins and notes of the *Bible de Jérusalem*.

La Bible de Jérusalem. La Sainte Bible, traduite en français sous la direction de l'Ecole biblique de Jérusalem. Nouvelle edition entièrement revue et augmentée. Paris, Cerf, 1988.
La Bibbia di Gerusalemme. Ed. F. VATTIONI. Bologna, Dehoniane, [7]1986.
The New Jerusalem Bible. London, Longman, 1991.
Nueva Biblia de Jerusalén. Revisada y aumentada. Bilbao, Desclée de Brouwer, 1989.
Neue Jerusalemer Bibel. Ed. A. DEISSLER – A. VÖGTLE. Freiburg, Herder, [3]1988.

The *Synopses* provide the possibility of a single grasp of parallel texts of the three 'synoptic' gospels:

K. ALAND, *Synopsis quattuor Evangeliorum*. Locis parellelis evangeliorum apocryphorum et patrum adhibitis. Stuttgart, Württembergische Bibelanstalt, [11]1980. [Greek text].
A. HUCK – H. GREEVEN, *Synopse der drei ersten Evangelien mit Beigabe der johannischer Parallelstellen*. Tübingen, Mohr, [13]1981. [Greek text, with titles also in English].
J.B. ORCHARD, *A Synopsis of the Four Gospels in Greek*, arranged according to the Two-Gospel Hypothesis. Edinburgh, Clarcke, 1983.
H.F.D. SPARKS, *A Synopsis of the Gospels*. The Synoptic Gospels with the Johannine Parallels. London, Black, 1964.
R.J. SWANSON, *The horizontal line synopsis of the Gospels*. Dillsboro NC, Western North Carolina Press, 1975.

M.J. LAGRANGE, *Sinossi dei quattro vangeli*. Brescia, Morcelliana, [8]1983.

J. SCHMID, *Sinossi dei tre primi Evangeli con i passi paralleli di Giovanni*. Brescia, Morcelliana, 1970.

A. POPPI, *Sinossi didattico-pastorale dei quattro vangeli*. 2 vol. Padova, Messaggero, [7]1986-1988 [one volume contains a commentary].

P. BENOIT – M.-E. BOISMARD, *Synopse des quatre Evangiles en français*. 3 vol. Paris, Cerf, 1972-1977 [consists of two volumes of literary comments].

The *Concordances* gather for every word all the places where it is found in Scripture:

F.J. ANDERSON - D. FORBES, *The Vocabulary of the Old Testament*. Roma, P.I. Biblico, 1989.

K. ALAND, *Vollständige Konkordanz zum griechischen Neuen Testament*. 3 vol. Berlin, Gruyter, 1978-1983.

W.R. MOULTON – A.S. GEDEN, *A Concordance to the Greek Testament*. Edinburgh, Clark, [5]1978.

A. SCHMOLLER, *Concordantiae Novi Testamenti Graeci*. Handkonkordanz zum griechischen Neuen Testament. Stuttgart, Württembergische Bibelanstalt, [14]1968.

Computer-Kondordanz zum Novum Testamentum Graece von Nestle-Aland. Berlin, Gruyter, 1980.

B. FISCHER, *Novae Concordantiae bibliorum sacrorum iuxta vulgatam versionem critice editam*. 5 vol. Stuttgart, Frommann, 1977.

H. DE RAZE, alii, *Concordantiarum S. Scripturae manuale*. Ristampa Barcelona, Libreria Religiosa, 1951.

C. MORRISON, *An Analytical Concordance to the Revised Standard Version of the New Testament*. Philadelphia, Westminster Press, 1979.

M. BARDY, alii, *Concordance de la Bible. Nouveau Testament*. Paris, Cerf, 1970.

ID., *Le concordanze del Nuovo Testamento*. Torino, Marietti, 1978.

ID., *Concordancias de la Biblia. Nuevo Testamento*. Bilbao, Desclée de Brouwer – Mensajero, 1975.

G. PASSELECQ – F. POSWICK, *Table pastorale de la Bible*. Index analytique et analogique. Paris, Lethielleux, 1974.

ID., *Concordanza pastorale della Bibbia*. Bologna, Dehoniane,
1987.

Concordance de la Bible de Jérusalem, réalisée à partir de la
banque de données bibliques de l'abbaye de Maredsous.
Paris-Turnhout, Cerf-Brepols, 1982.

L. LUJAN, *Concordancias del Nuevo Testamento*. Barcelona,
Herder, 1975.

5.213 Among the innumerable *Commentaries* we indicate
only two which are particularly important because of the material they bring together:

For the Jewish context of the New Testament:

H.L. STRACK – P. BILLERBECK, *Kommentar zum Neuen Testament*
aus Talmud und Midrash. 6 vol. München, Beck, 1926-1961.

The comments of the Fathers of the Church are found in:

R. CORNELY and others, *Cursus Scripturae Sacrae*. 35 vol. Paris,
Lethielleux, 1885ss.

5.22 *Becoming familiar with the documents of the*
Magisterium: The authoritative teachings of the Magisterium
of the Church, whether more or less solemn, do not propose
'new' contents which theology must interpret, but rather the
very norms for theological *interpretation* of the word of God.
It is therefore necessary to become familiar with at least the
more important of these teachings (and not only with those of
Vatican II!), especially with those texts which are more frequently cited and commented upon in class, and to be able to
discern their exact meaning and their authority.

5.221 The *documents* themselves may be found in:

H. DENZINGER – A. SCHÖNMETZER, *Enchiridion Symbolorum,*
Definitionum et Declarationum de rebus fidei et morum.
Freiburg-Barcelona, Herder, [36]1976. [Cited as: DS].

ID., *El magisterio de la Iglesia. Manual de los Símbolos, Definiciones, y Declaraciones de la Iglesia en material de fé y costumbres.* Ed. D. RUIZ BUENO. Barcelona, Herder, [3]1963. [Translation of an earlier edition of Denzinger].

J. ALBERIGO, alii, *Conciliorum Oecumenicorum Decreta.* Bologna, Istituto Scienze Religiose, [3]1973.

H. RAHNER − K.H. WEGER, *Der Glaube der Kirche in den Urkunden der Lehrverkündigung.* Regensburg, Pustet, [11]1983.

J. NEUNER − H. ROOS, *La fede della Chiesa nei documenti del Magistero.* Ed. D. BALBONI. Roma, Studium, 1967. [Translation of an earlier edition of Rahner-Weger].

J. NEUNER − J. DUPUIS, *The Christian Faith in the Doctrinal Documents of the Catholic Church.* Bangalore, Theological Publications in India, [11]1991.

G. DUMEIGE, *Textes doctrinaux du Magistère de l'Eglise sur la foi catholique.* Paris, Orante, [4]1986.

ID., *La fé católica.* Textos doctrinales del magisterio de la Iglesia. Barcelona, Estela, 1956.

J. COLLANTES, *La fé de la Iglesia Católica.* Las ideas y los hombres en los documentos doctrinales del Magisterio. Madrid, BAC, [2]1984.

J.F. CLARKSON, alii. *The Church Teaches.* Documents of the Church in English Translation. London, Herder, [3]1960.

For the creeds, one may consult:

J.N.D. KELLY, *Early Christian Creeds.* London, Longman, [3]1972.

ID., *I simboli di fede della Chiesa Antica.* Napoli, Dehoniane, 1987.

ID., *Primitivos Credos Cristianos.* Salamanca, Secretariado Trinitario, 1980.

ID., *Alte christliche Glaubensbekenntnise.* Göttingen, Vandenhoeck, 1972.

The complete collection of all the *Acts of the Councils* may be found in:

G.D. MANSI, *Sacrorum Conciliorum nova et amplissima collectio.* 53 vol. Firenze-Venezia-Paris, Welter, 1759-1927; Graz, Akademie, 1960-62.

Further indications may be found in:

M. CHAPPIN, *Strumenti di lavoro per la teologia*. Roma, P.U. Gregoriana, 1990, pp. 65-67.

5.222 For the *interpretation* of these documents we do not as yet have tools which are sound and handy. Still, one could consult:

W. BEINERT, Der "Denzinger", in: ID., *Dogmatik studieren*. Regensburg, Pustet, 1985, p. 179-197.

P. PALAZZINI, *Dizionario dei Concili*. 6 vol. Roma, P.U. Lateranense Ist. Giovanni XXIII, 1963-68.

H. JEDIN, *Kleine Konziliengeschichte*. Mit einem Bericht über das Zweite Vatikanische Konzil. Freiburg, Herder, [5]1986.

ID., *Breve storia dei Concili*. I ventuno concili ecumenici nel quadro della storia della Chiesa. Brescia, Morcelliana, [6]1983.

ID., *Ecumenical Councils of the Catholic Church*. A historical outline. London, Nelson, 1960.

G. DUMEIGE (ed.), *Histoire des Conciles Oecuméniques*. 12 vol. Paris, Orante, 1962-80.

ID., H. BACHT, *Geschichte der ökumenischen Konzilien*. 12 vol. Mainz, Grünewald, 1963-85.

ID., *Historia de los Concilios Ecuménicos*. 3 volumes to date. Vitoria, Eset, 1969-

For the Council of Trent:

H. JEDIN, *Geschichte des Konzils von Trient*. 5 vol. Freiburg, Herder, [3]1976-78.

ID., *Storia del Concilio de Trento*. 5 vol. Brescia, Morcelliana, [2]1973-82.

ID., *A History of the Council of Trent*. 2 vol. London, Nelson, 1957-61 [translation incomplete].

ID., *Historia del Concilio de Trento*. 4 vol. Pamplona, Univ. de Navarra, 1961.

ID., *Histoire du Concile de Trente*. Paris, Desclée, 1965-

A. MICHEL, *Les décrets du Concile de Trente*. (HEFELE-LECLERCQ, *Historie des Conciles d'après les documents originaux*, vol. X, 1). Paris, Letouzey, 1938.

For Vatican Council I:

J.M.A. VACANT, *Etudes théologiques sur les Constitutions du Concile du Vatican, d'après les Actes du Concile.* 2 vol. Paris-Lyon, Delhomme, 1895.
De doctrina Concilii Vaticani primi. Studia selecta annis 1948-64 scripta. Roma, Vaticana, 1969.
Cf. also the articles in DTC and LThK (cf. below 5.313). For vatican Council II consult M. CHAPPIN, *op. cit.,* pp. 68-71.

5.23 *Making contact with Tradition,* in an anthological and representative way. The worth of a theologian is in direct proportion to his or her knowledge of Tradition, because he or she must insert himself or herself into it, and from it derive *fertile suggestions* for the contemporary interpretation of the word of God. Even the documents of the Magisterium have their precise meaning only within the context of Tradition.

It would however be utopian to want to familarize oneself with the whole of Tradition during the first years of study. But here is a *reasonable way of proceeding*: after having dedicated oneself in the beginning to a study of Sacred Scripture, in another year one could concentrate, in personal study, on a personal contact with the Fathers (or even one year for the study of the Greek Fathers, and another year for the Latin Fathers), and in a third year on medieval theology. For such a study one should read: a *compendium* of patrology and/or of the history of dogma (for having a panoramic view); *an original work* (chosen in consultation with the professor); and *anthologically*, some of the more important texts to which the course or textbook make reference.

One can find a brief panorama of the history of dogma in:

H. RONDET, *Histoire du dogma.* Tournai, Desclée, 1971.
ID., *Storia del dogma.* Bari, Ecumenica, 1973.

For patristics, the best compendiums are:

B. ALTANER – A. STUIBER, *Patrologie.* Leben, Schriften und Lehre der Kirchenväter. Freiburg, Herder, [9]1980.

ID., *Patrologia*. Torino, Marietti, 1981.
ID., *Patrology*. Freiburg, Herder, 1960.
ID., *Précis de patrologie*, ed. H. CHIRAT. Mulhouse, Salvator, 1961.
I. QUASTEN, *Patrology*. 4 vol. Utrecht, Spectrum, 1983.
ID., *Patrologia*. 3 vol. Torino, Marietti, [2]1980-81.
ID., *Patrologia*. 3 vol. Madrid, BAC, [4]1985.
ID., *Initiation aux Pères de l'Eglise*. 4 vol. Paris, Cerf, 1955-88.

Abundant information may be found in:

A. DI BERNARDINO, *Dizionario patristico e di antichitá cristiane*. 3 vol. Casale Monferrato, Marietti, 1983-88.
ID., *Dictionnaire encyclopédique du christianisme ancien*. 2 vol. Paris, Cerf, 1990.

For the history of theology one may consult:

E. VILANOVA, *Historia de la teología cristiana*. 2 volumes to date. Barcelona, Herder, 1967-89.
G.R. EVANS – A.E. MCGRATH – A.D. GALLOWAY, *The History of Christian Theology*. Vol. I. The Science of Theology. Grand Rapids MI, Eerdmans, 1986.
B. HÄGGLUND, *Geschichte der Theologie*. Ein Abriss. München, Kaiser, 1983.
M. GRABMANN, *Die Geschichte der katholischen Theologie seit dem Ausgang der Väterzeit*. Freiburg, Herder, 1933. Darmstadt, Wiss. Buchgesellschaft, 1980.
Besides these, one may consult the *Compendi di storia di un singolo dogma*, which will be listed below in 5.32.

An anthology of patristic texts which, though insufficient, permit a first contact with the texts themselves, may be found in:

M. ROUËT DE JOURNEL, *Enchiridion Patristicum*. Loci SS. Patrum, Doctorum, Scriptorum Ecclesiasticorum in usum scholarum. Freiburg-Barcelona, Herder, [24]1968.

For the *editions of texts* of the Fathers of the Church (and of the medieval theologians), see M. CHAPPIN, *op. cit.*, (5.221) pp. 78-85.

NB: For *philosophy* there are no *normative* texts as in theology. However, what we have said about theological Tradition is valid analogically also for philosophy: the worth also of a philosopher stands in direct proportion to his knowledge of the great philosophers. It is therefore necessary to familarize oneself with these, proceeding in the way described for theological Tradition. One must read above all *some of the most important texts* of the great philosophers which are referred to in the courses, and in the first place the texts of *St. Thomas Aquinas.*

PRACTICAL EXERCISES: 1. Read in context the biblical and magisterial texts cited in a chapter of the textbook. What does such a contextual vision add?

2. Collect the parallel texts which refer to some biblical (or New Testament) theme.

3. (For philosophers): Read and discuss in common some text of St. Thomas cited in the courses.

5.3 *Filling in historical information*

Given the importance of these sources, which are all historical in character, a good part of the teaching of theology and philosophy consists of *historical information* (dates, facts, doctrines). However such information (names, technical terms, etc.) often receives only a bare mention in the lectures and textbooks; the task of *filling in* this information and *making it more precise* is left to personal study. It is therefore necessary:

5.31 *To gather supplementary information* on the authors or currents of thought which are cited: Who are they? When did the author live? What has he written? To what current or school did he belong? What are his principal doctrines? Does he use any peculiar terminology? And for currents of thought: Who are its representatives? How did it arise? What is its historical importance? All this, not in order to satisfy idle curiosity (the so-called 'erudition'), but for the sake of *understand-*

ing better, attaching *a precise historical significance* to names and technical terms.

The required information can be found: first of all by using the *Index of names* of the textbook (is the same author spoken of elsewhere? What is said about him?); next by reading the corresponding article or articles in some *Encyclopedia.* In this case, one begins always with some *brief* article (in a *specialized Dictionary,* or in a *general Encyclopedia,* cf. also 5.11 above), taking note of the *cross-references,* and only later, if the matter seems interesting and important enough, to the more substantial articles found in the *specialized Encyclopedias.*

5.311 *General encyclopedias* which provide information also in philosophical and theological matters:

Enciclopedia Italiana. Grande Dizionario Enciclopedico. Lessico Universale Italiano. Enciclopedia Einaudi. Encyclopedia Britannica. Gran Enciclopedia Rialp (GER). Verbo, Enciclo-pédia Luso-Brasileira, etc.

Particularly fruitful is the consultation of Encyclopedias (specialized or semi-specialized) *close* to our disciplines:

Enciclopedia Cattolica. 12 vol. Firenze, Sansoni, 1948-54.
[Completed by: S. GAROFALO, *Dizionario del Concilio Ecumenico Vaticano Secondo.* Roma, Unedì, 1969].
Dizionario Ecclesiastico. 3 vol. Torini, UTET, 1953-58.
Encyclopaedia of Religion and Ethics. 12 vol. Edinburgh, 1908-21.
New Catholic Encyclopedia. 15 vol. + 3 suppl. New York, McGraw, 1967-89.
Enciclopedia de la Religión Católica. 7 vol. Barcelona, Dalman, 1956.
Catholicisme. Hier, aujourd'hui, demain. 12 volumes to date. Paris, Letouzey, 1948-
Encyclopaedia Universalis. 22 vol. Paris, Encycl. Univ., [2]1985-86.
[A general French encyclopedia, with supplementary volumes issued every year. The philosophical articles here are particularly good.]

Staatslexikon. Recht, Wirtschaft, Gesellschaft. 8 vol. Freiburg, Herder, [6]1957-63.

Der kleine Pauly Lexikon der Antike. 5 vol. Stuttgart, Druckenmühl, 1964-76.

5.312 *For philosophy*

Works for rapid consultation:

Dizionario dei filosofi, ed. Centro di Studi Filosofici di Gallarate. Firenze, Sansoni, 1976 [An extraction of basic articles from the 'Enciclopedia filosofica'].

Dizionario dei filosofi del Novecento. Firenze, Olschki, 1985. [Extracted from the 'Enciclopedia filosofica', with additions].

I. SORGI, *Dizionario di Filosofia.* Gli autori, le correnti, I concetti, le opere. Milano, Rizzoli, 1976.

G.H.R. PARKINSON, *An Encyclopedia of Philosophy.* London, Routledge, 1989.

D.D. RUNES, *Who's Who in Philosophy.* New York, Greenwood, [2]1969. [On philosophers living in 1942, date of the first edition].

ID., *Dizionario di filosofia.* Milano, Mondadori, [6]1982.

J.O. URMSON, *The Concise Encyclopedia of Western Philosophy and Philosophers.* London, Hutchinson, [2]1975.

ID., *Encyclopedia concise de filosofia y filósofos.* Madrid, Cattedra, 1979.

S. AROUX – Y. WEIL, *Dictionnaire des auteurs et des thèmes de la philosophie.* Paris, Hachette, 1975.

D. HUISMANS (ed.). *Dictionnaire des Philosophes.* 2 vol. Paris, PUF, 1984. [Specially for the more recent philosophers; articles by authors of great renown].

P. JERPHAGNON, *Dictionnaire des grandes philosophies.* Paris, Privat, 1973.

Dictionnaire illustré des philosophes. Parish, Seghers, 1962.

F. VOLPI, *Lexicon der philosophischen Werke.* Stuttgart, Kröner, 1988.

W. ZEIGENFUSS, *Philosophen-Lexikon.* Handwörterbuch der Philosophie nach Personen. Berlin, Gruyter, 1949-50.

Larger specialized encyclopedias:

Enciclopedia filosofica, ed. Centro di Studi Filosofici di Gallarate, 8 vol., Roma, Lucarini, [3]1982. [Now sold under the title: *Dizionario enciclopedico di filosofia*].

P. EDWARDS, *Encyclopedia of Philosophy.* 4 vol. New York, Free Press, ²1973; popular edition, London, Macmillan, 1972.

J. FERRATER MORA, *Diccionario de filosofía.* 4 vol. Madrid, Alianza, ⁴1982.

A. JACOB (ed.), *Encyclopédie Philosophique Universelle.* 3 volumes to date: I. L'universe philosophique. II, 1-2. Les notions philosophiques. Dictionnaire. Paris, PUF, 1989- [The 'Dictionnaire' includes also the oriental philosophies and Greek, Arab, Hebrew terminology...].

J. MITTELSTRASS, *Encyklopädie Philosophie und Wissenschaftstheorie.* 2 volumes to date. Mannheim, B.I. – Wissenschaftsverlag, 1980-

H.J. SANDKÜHLER (ed.), *Europäische Encyklopädie zu Philosophie und Wissenschaften.* 4 volumes to date. Hamburg, Meiner, 1991-

A special mention is due to a work which has just been begun and which will become an indispensable point of reference:

R. GOULET, *Dictionnaire des philosophes antiques.* 1 volume to date. (Abammon to Axiotléa). Paris, Editions du CNRS, 1989-

5.313 *For theology* there are at present six great specialized *Encyclopedias* (three Catholic and three non-Catholic, which always contain also philosophical articles):

Dictionnaire de Théologie Catholique, containing expositions of Catholic theological doctrines, their proofs and their history. 33 vol. Paris, Letouzey, 1902-72. [Cited as: DTC; the last three volumes of *Tables Générales* contain also additions and updates].

Lexikon für Theologie und Kirche. 2. Aufl. 14 vol. Freiburg, Herder, 1957-68. [Cited as: LThK²; the three volumes contain an annotated edition of the documents of Vatican Council II].

A Catholic Dictionary of Theology, ed. J. CREHAN, 4 volumes to date. London, Nelson, 1962-

Evangelisches Kirchenlexikon. Internationale theologische Encyklopädie. 2 volumes to date. Göttingen, Vandenhoeck, ³1986-

Die Religion in Geschichte und Gegenwart. Handwörterbuch für Theologie und Religionswissenschaft. 3. Aufl. 7 vol. Tübingen,

Mohr, 1957-64. [Cited as: RGG[3]: Protestant, but reliable also as far as the Catholic entries are concerned, and above all for the philosophical entries]
Theologische Realenzyklopädie. 20 volumes to date + *Abkürzungsverzeichnis*, ed. S. SCHWERTNER (1976). Berlin, Gruyter, 1977- [Cited as: TRE].

Besides these:

O. DE LA BROSSE, *Dictionnaire de la foi chrétienne.* 2 vol. Paris, Cerf, 1968 [The second volume contains useful historical tables].

ID., *Nuovo dizionario del cristianesimo.* Brescia, Queriniana, 1971.

H.J. SCHULTZ, *Tendenzen der Theologie im 20. Jahrhundert.* Eine Geschichte in Porträts. Stuttgart, Kreuz-Verlag, 21967 [Not an encyclopedia, but about a hundred biographical sketches; Protestant, but presents also the main Catholic theologians].

ID., *Lessico dei teologi del secolo XX.* (Mysterium Salutis, vol. 12). Brescia, Queriniana, 1978.

5.314 Besides these, there are several encyclopedias for *particular theological disciplines*, mostly in French and still in the process of publication (*Dictionnaire de Spiritualité, Dictionnaire de Droit Canonique, Dictionnaire d'Histoire Ecclésiastique, Dictionnaire d'Archéologie chrétienne et de Liturgie...*). Among these, the *Enciclopedie di Scienze bibliche* is very useful, because it contains all the historical, archaeological, geographical and other information regarding Sacred Scripture and the biblical world:

Dictionnaire de la Bible. Supplément. 8 volumes to date. Paris, Letouzey, 1928- [Cited as: DBS or SDB].

E. GALBIATI, *Dizionario enciclopedico della Bibbia e del mondo biblico.* Milano, Massimo, 21988.

L. MONLOUBOU – F.M. DI BUIT, *Dizionario biblico storico-critico.* Roma, Borla, 1987.

P.J. ACHTEMEIER, *Harper's Bible Dictionary.* San Francisco, Harper, 1985.

R.J. COGGINS – J.L. HOULDEN, *A Dictionary of Biblical Inerpretation*. London, SCM Press, 1990.

The Interpreter's Dictionary of the Bible. 5 vol. New York, Abingdon, 1962-76.

J.L. MCKENZIE, *Dictionary of the Bible*. Milwaukee, Bruce, 1973.

ID., *Dizionario biblico*. Ed. B. MAGGIONI. Assisi, Cittadella, ^{4}1981.

Dictionnaire encyclopédique de la bible. Turnhout, Brepols, 1987.

Enciclopedia de la biblia. 6 vol. Barcelona, Exito, ^{2}1969.

Enciclopedia de la bibbia. 6 vol. Torino, ElleDiCi, 1969-71. [Translation of the Spanish encyclopedia].

H. HAAG, *Bibel-Lexikon*. Einsiedeln, Benziger, ^{2}1968. [The Italian translation: *Dizionario biblico*. Torino, SEI, 1960, is from the first edition, which is theologically less sound].

ID., *Diccionario de la Biblia*. Barcelona, Herder, ^{6}1971.

BO REICKE – L. ROST, *Biblisch-historisches Handwörterbuch*. Landeskunde, Geschichte, Religion, Kultur, Literatur. 4 vol. Göttingen, Vandenhoeck, 1962-79.

5.32 *To insert into a general historical horizon* the particular information received and gathered, so that we are not left with scattered and abstract notions (notionalism). To do this, it is necessary to obtain a *panoramic vision* of the historical horizon of the philosophy (history of thought) and theology (history of dogma) from the very beginning of one's studies. As far as *philosophy* is concerned, there are courses in history of philosophy which many may have taken in a more or less thorough way already in high school; those who have not done this should, in the first few months of study, read a *brief compendium* of this history.

For *theology* there are courses on the history of the Church and on patrology, but there is no course that deals strictly speaking with the history of dogmas and of post-patristic theology. One must fill in such a lacuna, reading at least for one or other of the more important treatises also a *compendium of the history of dogma* (where such compendiums exist!). Aids:

M. SCHMAUS, alii, *Handbuch der Dogmengeschichte.* 40 fascicles to date. Freiburg, Herder, 1951-

ID., *Histoire des dogmes.* 12 volumes to date. Paris, Cerf, 1966-

ID., *Historia de los dogmas.* 10 fascicles to date. Madrid, BAC, 1973-

A. DULLES, *A History of Apologetics.* London-New York, Hutchinson, 1971.

R. AUBERT, *Le problème de l'acte de foi.* Données traditionnelles et resultants des controverses récentes. Louvain-Paris, Nauwelaerts, ⁴1969.

A. GRILLMEIER, *Die theologische und sprachliche Vorbereitung der christologischen Formeln von Chalkedon,* in: ID., *Das Konzil von Chalkedon.* Geschichte und Gegenwart. Würzburg, Echter, ⁵1979. vol. I, pp. 5-202.

ID., *Christ in Christian Tradition* from the Apostolic Age to Chalcedon (451). London-Oxford, Mowbrays, ²1975.

ID., *Le Christ dans la tradition chrétienne*; de l'âge apostolique à Chalcédoine (451). Paris, Cerf, 1973.

A. GRILLMEIER, *Jesus der Christus im Glauben der Kirche.* 2 volumes to date. Freiburg, Herder, 1979 [Re-elaboration of the preceding work].

ID., *Gesù il Cristo nella fede della Chiesa.* 2 volumes to date. Brescia, Paideia, 1982.

TH. DE REGNON, *Études de théologie positive sur la Sainte Trinité.* 4 vol. Paris, Retaux, 1892-98.

J. LEBRETON, *Histoire du Dogme de la Trinité.* 2 vol. Paris, Beauchesne, 1919-28.

D. SPADA, *Le formule trinitarie.* Da Nicea a Costantinopoli. Roma, P.U. Urbaniana, 1988.

J. RIVIÈRE, *Le dogme de la redemption.* Essai d'étude historique. Paris, Lecoffre, 1905.

L. RICHARD, *Le mystère de la redemption.* Tournai, Desclée, 1959.

H. RONDET, *Gratia Christi.* Essai d'histoire du dogme et de théologie dogmatique. Paris, Beauchesne, 1948.

ID., *La grazia di Cristo.* Saggio di storia del dogma e di teologia dogmatica. Roma, Città Nuova, 1966.

H. RONDET, *Le péché original dans la tradition patristique et théologique.* Paris, Fayard, 1967.

ID., *Il peccato originale.* Roma, Borla, 1971.

ID., *Original Sin.* The patristic and theological background. Staten Island, Alba, 1972.

G. BARDY, *La théologie de l'Eglise*. De saint Clément de Rome à saint Irénée. Paris, Cerf, 1945. De saint Irénée au concile du Nicée. Ibid., 1947.

P. POURRAT, *La théologie sacramentaire*. Étude de théologie positive. Paris, Lecoffre, [4]1910.

H. GRAEF, *Maria*. Eine Geschichte der Lehre und Verehrung. Freiburg, Herder, 1964.

W. BEINERT – H. PETRI, *Handbuch der Marienkunde*. Regensburg, Pustet, 1984.

Other snippets of the history of dogmas may be found in the *specialized Encyclopedias* (see above 5.313).

PRACTICAL EXERCISES: 1. Gather information on a philosopher or theologian. Make a scheda.

2. Read the same article in different Encyclopedias; compare the information thus gathered. How would you characterize each of these Encyclopedias?

5.4 *Rethinking doctrines*

Philosophy and theology are not only a new language or a collection of historical information, but above all a *thoughtful, methodical, reasoned discourse* on the meaning of life and on the ultimate 'why' of all experiences. One does not appropriate such a discourse by repeating it like a parrot, without understanding its elements. It is necessary to *re-think it for oneself*, making it re-emerge from one's own depths, enriched and personalized.

To initiate such a re-thinking of philosophical or theological discourse — which must subsequently continue throughout one's life — the following 'speculative exercises' may be useful:

5.41 *Concretizing the concepts*. Every discourse is founded on the *meanings which are attached to words*, i.e. upon concepts. For an initial understanding of a discourse, a minimal and 'abstract' knowledge of the concepts used is enough; if instead one wishes to re-think it, one must have concepts *whose meaning is so 'concrete'* that it is able to regulate the use of this concept: which are the virtualities and the connections, which are the implications, the nuances, etc. To concretize in this way the concepts of philosophical and theological discourse, one may:

5.411 *Find out about their origin and history,* so that one may see them in the light of the whole of their past. The use of each of our words depends in fact on a whole linguistic tradition. It would be useful to re-trace it at least for a few key concepts, consulting, besides the already mentioned histories of thought and of dogma (5.32 above), also the specialized *historical Dictionaries:*

For *philosophy:*

A. LALANDE, *Vocabulaire technique et critique de la philosophie.* Paris, PUF, [17]1991. [A very authoritative work, fruit of the collaboration of very famous French philosophers; the dictionary refers their observations to individual words.]

ID., *Dizionario critico di filosofia.* Milano, ISEDI, [2]1975.

R. EISLER, *Wörterbuch der philosophischen Begriffe.* 3 vols. Berlin, Mittler, [4]1927-30. [Gathers, in great abundance, only the material: definitions given by different philosophers.]

J. RITTER, *Historisches Wörterbuch der Philosophie.* 7 vols. upto now. Basel-Stuttgart, Schwabe, 1971- [Elaborates the material given in Eisler into a proper 'Begriffsgeschichte'.]

Other indications may be found in the great philosophical Encyclopedias (see above 5.312).

For *theology* we must note above all the various *biblical Dictionaries,* of different sizes and character, which allow the development of a 'biblical theme':

G. KITTEL, *Theologisches Wörterbuch zum Neuen Testament.* 10 vol. Stuttgart, Kohlhammer, 1933-78. [A monumental work, fruit of the labours of the best German Protestant exegetes. Cited as: TWNT].

ID., *Theological Dictionary of the New Testament*. Ed. G.W. BROMILEY. 9 vol. Grand Rapids MI, Eerdmans, 1964-1974.

ID., *Grande Lessico del Nuovo Testamento*. Ed. F. MONTAGNINI – G. SCARPAT. 14 volumes to date. Brescia, Paideia, 1965-

H. BALZ – G. SCHNEIDER, *Exegetisches Wörterbuch zum Neuen Testament*. 3 vol. Stuttgart, Kohlhammer, 1980-83. [Based on the Greek text; an updating of KITTEL].

P. ROSSANO – G. RAVASI – A. GHIRLANDA, *Nuovo Dizionario di Teologia biblica*. Torino, Paoline, 1988.

X. LÉON-DUFOUR, *Dictionnaire du Nouveau Testament*. Paris, Seuil, 1975.

ID., *Dizionario del Nuovo Testamento*. Brescia, Queriniana, 1978.

ID., *Dictionary of the New Testament*. San Francisco, Harper, 1980.

ID., *Wörterbuch zum Neuen Testament*. München, Kösel, 1977.

J. MATEOS – J. BARRETO, *Vocabulario teológico del Evangelio de Juan*. Madrid, Cristianidad, 1988.

ID., *Dizionario teologico del Vangelo di Giovanni*. Assisi, Cittadella, 1982.

L. COENEN (ed.), *Theologisches Begriffslexikon zum Neuen Testament*. 2 vol. Wuppertal, Brockhaus, 1965-71.

ID., *Dizionario dei concetti biblici del Nuovo Testamento*. Bologna, Dehoniane, ²1980.

ID., *The New International Dictionary of New Testament Theology*. Ed. C. BROWN. 3 vol. Exeter, Paternoster, 1975-77.

ID., *Diccionario Teológico del Nuevo Testamento*. 4 vol. Barcelona, Sigueme, 1980-87.

C.J. BOTTERWECK – H. RINGGREN, *Theologisches Wörterbuch zum Alten Testament*. 6 volumes to date. Stuttgart, Kohlhammer, 1973- [accessible only to those with some knowledge of Hebrew].

ID., *Grande Lessico dell'Antico Testamento*. Brescia, Paideia, 1988- [only one volume to date].

ID., *Theological Dictionary of the Old Testament*. Grand Rapids MI, Eerdmans, 1977-

ID., *Diccionario Teológico del Antiguo Testamento*. 1 volume to date. Madrid, Cristianidad, 1973-

E. JENNI – C. WESTERMANN, *Theologisches Handwörterbuch zum Alten Testament*. 2 vol. München-Zürich, Kaiser-EVZ, 1971-75 [can be consulted even with very little knowledge of Hebrew].

ID., *Dizionario teologico dell'Antico Testamento.* 2 vol. Torino, Marietti, 1978-82.

W SCHMIDT, *Wörterbuch zur Bible.* Stuttgart, Kohlhammer, 1971 [Protestant].

ID., *Dizionario biblico.* Teologia dell'Antico Testamento. Milano, Jaca Book, 1981.

J.J. VON ALLMEN, *Vocabulaire biblique.* Neuchâtel-Paris, Delachaux, 1954 [Protestant].

ID., *Vocabolario biblico.* Roma, AVE, 1969.

ID., *Vocabulary of the Bible.* London, Lutterworth, 1958.

X. LÉON-DUFOUR, *Vocabulaire de théologie biblique.* Paris, Cerf, [2]1970 [Catholic; useful and handy].

ID., *Dizionario di teologia biblica.* Torino, Marietti, 1980.

ID., *Dictionary of Biblical Theology.* London, Chapman, [2]1973.

ID., *Vocabulario de Teología Bíblica.* Barcelona, Herder, [2]1973.

Dictionnaire des themes bibliques. Saint André, Abbaye de Saint André, 1974.

J.B. BAUER, *Bibeltheologisches Wörterbuch.* Graz, Styria, [3]1976. [Catholic, less reliable than Léon-Dufour].

ID., *Dizionario di teologia biblica.* Brescia, Morcelliana, 1969.

ID., *Sacramentum Verbi. An Encyclopedia of Biblical Theology.* 3 vol. London, Sheed, [2]1976.

ID., *Diccionario de Theología Bíblica.* Barcelona, Herder, 1967.

As far as the development of theological terminology is concerned, however, we do not as yet have a specialized Dictionary; pertinent indications may be found in the theological Encyclopedias (see above 5.313).

5.412 *Note the systematic connections* of the principal concepts. Their use is not normally limited to the context in which they are found the first time. One must therefore trace, mentally, the *constellation of possible meanings* of a word-concept, making use of the *systematic Dictionaries:*

For *philosophy:*

Dizionario delle idee, ed. del Centro Studi Filosofici di Gallarate. Firenze, Sansoni, 1977 (extracted from the *Enciclopedia filosofica*).

N. ABBAGNANO, *Dizionario di Filosofia*. Torino, UTET, ³1971.

A. NOIRAY, *La Philosophie*. Paris, Centre d'Études, 1969. [Specially for the more recent problematics].

A. MILLAN-PUELLES, *Léxico filosófico*. Madrid, Rialp, 1984.

H. KRINGS, alii, *Handbuch philosophischer Grundbegriffe*. 6 vol. München, Kösel, 1973-74.

ID., *Concetti fondamentali di filosofia*. 3 vol. Brescia, Queriniana, 1981-82.

ID., *Conceptos fundamentales de filosofia*. 3 vol. Barcelona, Herder, 1977-79.

For *theology*:

Sacramentum Mundi. Theologisches Lexikon für die Praxis. 4 vol. Freiburg, Herder, 1967-70.

ID., *Sacramentum Mundi*. An Encyclopaedia of Theology. 6 vol. London, Burns, 1968-70.

ID., *Sacramentum Mundi*. Enciclopedia teologica. 8 vol. Brescia, Morcelliana, 1974-77.

ID., *Sacramentum Mundi*. Enciclopedia teológica. 6 vol. Barcelona, Herder, 1972-76.

Shorter and updated version: *Encyclopedia of Theology*. A concise Sacramentum Mundi. London, Burns, 1975.

J.B. BAUER – C. MOLARI, *Dizionario teologico*. Assisi, Cittadella, 1974 [The subtitle of the German original reads: "Burning points from A to Z"].

L. PACOMIO, and others, *Dizionario teologico interdisciplinare*, 4 vol. Torino, Marietti, ²1982 [Besides the alphabetical dictionary, this contains also a systematic introduction and conclusion].

ID., *Diccionario teológico interdisciplinar*. 3 vol. Salamanca, Sigueme, 1982-85.

Dizionario dei temi della fede. Torino, SEI, 1977.

J. DORÉ, *Dictionnaire de théologie chrétienne*. Les grands thèmes de la foi. Paris, Desclée, 1979 [translation of the preceding item].

A. RICHARDSON – J. BOWDEN, *A New Dictionary of Christian Theology*. London, SCM Press, 1983 [Protestant].

J. LYON, *Les 50 mots-clefs de la théologie moderne*. Toulouse, Privat, 1970.

ID., *Le 50 parole-chiave della teologia moderna*. Roma, Paoline, 1972.

W. BEINERT (ed.), *Lexikon der katholischen Dogmatik*. Freiburg, Herder, 1987 [Interesting reflections].

ID., *Lessico di Teologia sistematica*. Brescia, Queriniana, 1990.

P. EICHER, *Neues Handbuch theologischer Grundbegriffe*. 4 vol. München, Kösel, 1984-85 [few articles, but substantial].

ID., *Enciclopedia teologica*. 4 vol. Brescia, Queriniana, 1989.

E. FAHLBUSCH, *Taschenlexikon Religion und Theologie*. 5 vol. Göttingen, Vandenhoeck, [4]1983 [Protestant].

H. FRIES, *Handbuch theologischer Grundbegriffe*. 2 vol. München, Kösel, 1962-63. Pocketbook edition: 4 vol. DTV, 1970.

ID., *Dizionario teologico*. Ed. G. RIVA, 3 vol. Brescia, Queriniana, 1979.

ID., *Encyclopédie de la foi*. Paris, Cerf, 1965-66.

H. RAHNER, alii. *Herders theologisches Taschenlexikon*. (Herderbücherei, 451-58). 8 vol. Freiburg, Herder, 5[1980] [Extract from LThK[2] and "Sacramentum Mundi"].

5.42 *Note the connections.* Simply by paying attention to the *recurrence of the same words*, concepts or types of arguments in the various philosophical or theological disciplines, every student must be able to compose, by himself, a sort of 'summula' or brief synthesis of philosophy and of theology. In fact, the object of philosophy and of theology being fundamentally *one* (in contrast to the multiple objects of the sciences) there is among their various disciplines a *convergence* that is far more marked that what the individual courses make evident.

Therefore it will be the task of every student *to pay attention to the convergences,* the parallelisms, the connections between the different subjects that he studies. In this way there will gradually emerge in his spirit that *personal synthesis* which reflects the unity of philosophy and of theology.

5.43 *Personalize the discourse.* A discourse (even a philosophical or theological one) is not something immanent, it is not merely a methodically coherent aggregate of concepts, but centers around an object, i.e. it speaks about an *experience*. Rethinking a discourse implies therefore rendering oneself capable of *expressing in one's own words* an experience which has become a *personal experience*. Only then can one say: "I know," and not merely "The professor says." How to arrive at this?

5.431 *Ask yourself what problem may be answered or personal experience illuminated* by that doctrine which you are studying. That is, ask yourself, for every philosophical or theological theme: "What does this mean *to me?*" This does not mean that a doctrine is significant only insofar as it "says something to me"; it means rather that I can *appropriate it*, rethink it, in its proper and full meaning, only in the measure that I have a question to which that doctrine responds. In this way the doctrines studied should make me turn my attention to many experiences and questions that I have till now neglected.

On such an experiential basis it will be possible:

5.432 *To express in your own words* the answers received from the doctrines you are studying — not only translating the terminology (as in 5.12 above), but *re-constructing and re-composing the entire discourse* by myself.

5.44 *To check the method.* While antiquity and the middle ages used to define a science by its object ("scientia ex causis"), in modern times the scientific character of a discourse is found in its *methodical rigor*: whether it proceeds according to logical rules in such a way that it can be checked and repeated by anybody at all. While personalizing a philosophical or theological discourse in the way discussed above (5.43) therefore, one must be careful to preserve the same methodical and critical rigor as the original discourse — because otherwise it would become merely an arbitrary 'opinion'. It is necessary therefore:

5.441 *To note the method followed by the professor* in his

discourse, studying especially his *logical rigor* (where the arguments are proposed in syllogistic form, such a check is at least formally easier), as well as the *critical value* of the initial data. The rules of logic and of historical criticism as well as the principal speculative methods will be taught in the introductory courses and especially in the seminars.

5.442 *To check your own discourse:* whether it is *coherent,* proceeding step by step according to the rules of logic; whether it is based on data that is critically dependable, without making 'extrapolations' (affirming more than what the premises allow); whether it is *intelligible,* developing according to a clear methodological scheme — or whether instead the sole guarantee and justification is "This is what I think". In such a case it would be good to open oneself to criticism by the group.

PRACTICAL EXERCISES: 1. For some particular concept, search: its historical origin, its systematic connections, its re-emergence in different treatises. Compile for it a sort of 'identity card'.
2. Ask yourself about the possible 'personalization' of some particular doctrine and discuss it in group.
3. During the discussion, check the methodical rigor of the arguments put forward.

5.5 *Writing a summary*

The fruit of such a private elaboration of material provided by the course and by the textbook should be a *brief written summary.*
— This serves as a *check on oneself,* because to have understood = to be able to say clearly;
— it amounts to *preserving,* in a condensed form, the results of personal study;
— it helps in the *preparation for the examination,* because it gives a synthetic vision and thus helps the memory.

5.51 *What should this summary contain?* In the *shortest possible form* one must write down *all that is essential* in a chapter of the textbook or of the course, adding the *most important results of personal study*. To condense in this way, in one or two pages (not too densely written), implies that the matter has been well 'digested': a good summary is always the *result of a personal re-elaboration*; it is not enough to transcribe, in a brief way, the text of the manual!

5.52 *How to write a summary.* Write on paper that is not too small in size (foolscap or half foolscap), always in a uniform manner, neatly and above all without cramming, so that it is *clearly legible* and can be fixed even visually in the memory. To help such 'visibility' one can also make use of (underlining in) different colors.

It is useful to proceed *always in the same order* (at least for the systematic subjects), e.g. after the title there could be a summary in a single proposition of the *essential content* of the chapter; next, one could indicate briefly the reason *why* this problem is discussed at this point; then the most important *notions* can be put together (with definitions, distinctions, explanations, indicating examples with a single key-word); then a brief sketch of the *history* of the problem (or of the *opinions* of other philosophers or theologians). Finally the *proofs* can be briefly mentioned (texts of Sacred Scripture, of the Magisterium, mentioning with some key-word the interpretations given; sketches of philosophical proofs). Cf. what was said above (2.23) on the structure of the scholastic 'thesis', with the further explanations given by Z. ALSZEGHY - M. FLICK, *Come si fa la teologia,* pp. 193-195.

Other material which has been gathered (on cards of smaller size) during personal study in order to illustrate or complete what is said in the text book, may simply be *inserted* into the folded paper of the summary, fixing the whole with a paper-clip.

5.53 *How to use the summaries.* Summaries are essentially a question of a *materialized memory*. Therefore they must be written when the matter is still fresh in the memory (never postpone the study of the systematic treatises to the end of the semester or of the year!), and must be *read* every now and then. (The psychological optimum for memorization is revision in arithmetical progression: 4, 8 days, 2, 4 weeks, 2, 4, 8 months ...). With such regular revision of summaries there is practically no need of further memorization before the examinations!

When later one finds other material which goes together with this or that summary, this can easily be added (and therefore make sure you leave enough space for such additions!).

Being merely a memory, the summary does *not* give sufficient basis for *revising* the same matter in a deeper way (e.g. in preparing an examination). For the *immediate preparation* of an examination one must go back also to the textbook or to the notes taken in class, but the summary will serve as guide.

NB: In the *organization of the time* dedicated to personal study, one must take into account two psychological exigences: one the one hand one must study the matter when it is still fresh, on the other hand one concentrates better when one studies the same matter for a longer period of time. The best compromise seems to be *to organize one's study in 'blocks'* of one, two or three weeks, dedicated exclusively or predominantly to the study of a particular subject, then passing on to another.

PRACTICAL EXERCISE: Make a summary of one chapter of some systematic treatise, under the supervision of the director of the proseminar.

6. The Examinations

Are examinations something good or are they a necessary evil? Whatever the answer, examinations are neither the goal nor the most important part of study. *Vitae, non examini discimus:* we study for *life*, not for examinations. The praxis of life will be the definitive *evaluation* of the theories studied: whether philosophy has nurtured a more conscious and rational attitude in the face of the great questions; whether theology has made possible a more comprehensive and more appropriate proclamation of the word of God.

It would however be presumptuous to wish to postpone all evaluation of the success of studies to the moment of actual practice: at that moment it is too late to remedy possible defects. There is need therefore, in the course of studies itself, of those *partial* (and somewhat artificial) *evaluations* which are the examinations.

The *student* verifies, in the "objectifying" presence of the examiner, his knowledge and understanding of the matter and his ability to express it. Besides, the examinations are an occasion for him, with a strong psychological stimulus, to revise, in a manner at once deeper and more synthetic, all that has been studied.

The *professor* checks in the first place the ordinary progress of the students, trying to discover whether there are any large gaps in their knowledge or in their understanding of the matter studied. In doing this, he also verifies the success of his own teaching, and receives a feedback which will help him improve it.

6.1 *Preparation for the examinations*

The preparation of an examination is done in two phases, remote and immediate. The first consists in personal study during the whole semester, as was described already. For the *immediate preparation*, it is necessary to *revise* the whole matter studied, *filling in the* gaps in memory and above all in understanding, using the means indicated in the previous chapter. Sometimes it may be useful and stimulating to read calmly ('meditatively') a chapter of a book or some good article about the matter which one is preparing. A frantic gathering of material and 'revisions' which are equally frantic are not helpful in preparing a good examination: they merely serve to disturb the calmness of the memory.

What is important therefore is to have done the *remote preparation* well, i.e. *to have studied regularly* throughout the semester. If this has been done, the immediate preparation requires little, and sometimes very little time. During the last weeks before the examination instead, it is absolutely impossible to make the necessary preparations. One therefore falls back upon a merely notionalistic memorization, which is a pure waste of time, because it does not yield any lasting and enduring knowledge.

All this is valid naturally only for the principal examinations; for the *secondary subjects and optional courses*, one should try not to waste too much time in preparing examinations which in the end 'count' for nothing (the 'credits' or coefficients give a good indication of the effort to be invested in the different examinations).

Immediately before an important examination, it is necessary above all to have the mind free and rested; a day of rest would therefore be more valuable than three days of frantic revision.

6.2 *The examination itself*

The examinations may be either oral or written, with characteristics (and techniques of examining) which are quite different:

6.21 *The oral examination*, because of the presence and repeated interventions of the examiner, is *more 'competitive'*. There is the possibility of asking and giving further explanations, of correcting or opening oneself to correction of mistaken answers, of beginning a deeper and more extended dialogue on some interesting point. The weaker student can *allow himself to be guided* step by step by the professor; also, there is always the possibility of passing to another question or theme if the student does not know anything about the first. The brilliant student can even *take over the initiative* in the dialogue. It is easier for the professor to understand the personality of the student, and he can therefore give a more balanced judgment; the student instead is often apprehensive and inhibited when he finds himself face to face with the professor.

A good beginning is important for success in an oral examination. In order to overcome at least the *initial moment of 'panic'* it is useful to have ready some general formula with which to begin the discourse (one could even make use of the paper containing the themes for the examination which is always kept on the examination table). One should not give the impression of reciting a text that one has learnt by heart. One should instead be always attentive to the precise question as it has been posed. One should also be prepared for the question with which many professors begin the examination: "ON which point would you like to be examined?" At any rate it is good to have prepared a brief (and as far as possible uniform) *scheme of exposition* on individual points. This enables one to speak intelligently (without trying to appear brilliant!) for a few minutes, before the professor can intervene with other questions.

Most students tend to overrate the role of *memory* in examinations, while the questions of the examiner are directed mostly at their *understanding*. It is not therefore necessary to have an answer "at the tip of the tongue", or to make the disk spin anxiously in one's mental computer. An examination is not a TV quiz, but rather a dialogue between intelligent persons. What is important is to *reflect* on the question posed, see its precise significance, situate it in a broader context, foresee connections and difficulties and possible answers. Thus, in the process of elaboration a *personal answer*, concentrating more on the real problem than on the words, slowly there will emerge also those data of memory which at first seemed to have been forgotten.

Giving the primacy to reflection (and sometimes to simple common sense!) rather than to memory, it is possible also to more easily avoid or to overcome that *'block'* in examinations which is the psychological fact of anxiety, caused not so much by tension and tiredness, as by the thought, "I don't know this!" This may be done by paying attention only to those contents which actually emerge in the memory. Again, one who knows that he does not know, is normally one who knows very well — even without being a Socrates. If therefore one is asked a question which, after reflection, one positively knows one cannot answer, it is better to say so immediately and to request the professor to pass on to some other question. Perhaps in the course of the dialogue the forgotten answer will re-emerge.

6.22 *The written examination* can be either in the form of a quiz, with short questions, or in the form of a dissertation, or else mixed. The advantage of the quiz form is that it allows a rapid check of the information assimilated, but if the questions are well chosen and formulated, it reveals also the level of comprehension of the student. The *answers* should be like the questions: *brief, concise and precise*, as 'objective' as possible. The dissertation, especially if the time given for the examination is long enough, reveals instead the level of personal assimilation, of comprehension and even of the creativity of the student. What is asked here is a *coherent discussion*, well structured and formulated, and even a *personal* one. To do well in this type of examination, it is not enough to merely reproduce the material given in the course.

More than the oral examination, the written examination offers the possibility of a *calm and prolonged reflection* and allows one to keep in mind all that is asked and to go over it again. The absence of the examiner reduces the moment of 'panic', but also does away with the possibility of finding out immediately whether one is right. *Before writing*, one should read the questions or the themes carefully and several times (so as not to misunderstand what is being asked), and for a dissertation one must make a *plan*; then, while writing, one should try to *formulate one's answer accurately*. For all this, it is useful to have acquired a habit of writing and composing. And one should not forget: the more *legible* the writing, the easier will it be for the professor to evaluate you positively.

6.23 *In general,* to do an examination well, one needs a bit of a *sporting spirit*, because it is a question of a real *competition*, where the student pits his own forces against those of another (the examiner). Fairness is needed of course, and a bit of aggressivity, but one must also know how to lose. The *result* is never an evaluation of the entire personality of the student, and not even of the whole of his student life (it would be completely unjust to make such an evaluation on the basis of a fifteen-minute examination), but it indicates only the measure of his performance in those fifteen minutes. It is quite possible that a good student sometimes fails an examination. On the other hand, doing well at the examinations is not enough to make one a good student.

The PRACTICAL EXERCISES will be the examinations themselves. But in order to have some preparation, one could:
— have a mock oral examination, and discuss the performance of the student;
— compose two or three pages in a fixed time as in a written examination, and discuss them.

PART FOUR

CREATIVE STUDY

One studies not merely to assimilate and to appropriate ready-made knowledge, but also with the hope of *utilizing* this knowledge and giving others *something new*. The goal of assimilative study is creative study; the limits between the two are fluid. Further, creative study must continue in some way throughout one's life, because it provides the basis, and is even itself a part of pastoral work.

In creative study also one follows a path that leads from a more *receptive* to a more *productive* type of work.

7. Reading

Creative study begins paradoxically from *reading* — because, as Vico says, "the human mind is like the earth, which however fertile it be, if it does not nourish itself with reading, becomes sterile in the end." In fact one can read either to collect information (5.3 above) or to assimilate a knowledge that has become traditional (2.2 above), but also in order to *stimulate one's thinking* — whether this is a question of making the effort to enter into the thought of another, or of being provoked by the text.

7.1 *What can and what must be read?*

The matter offered for our reading, even on a single problem, is vast, and the bibliographical indications given in courses and manuals are usually abundant. One has to make a *choice*, and one must distinguish *various degrees of intensity* in reading.

In order to make such a choice, first of all one must consider:

7.11 *The purpose for which one reads.* One can read for two quite different reasons, and these result in two types of reading which are almost opposed, not only in the choice of books, but also in the manner of reading.

7.111 *For the sake of information*, one reads to *keep oneself up to date*, where one may be:
— a cultured person of our time,
— a well-prepared priest (or lay catholic)
— a person with some concrete responsibility (e.g. studying philosophy, giving religious courses, being a parish priest, teaching in a seminary)
— a person faced with some particular task (e.g. a dissertation on Aristotelian physics, or a reading of St. Paul with high school students).

This list already indicates, in concentric circles as it were, the different grades of urgency of the informative reading (remembering however that urgency and importance do not coincide, but are often in competition).

7.112 *For the sake of formation* instead one reads in order to *enrich oneself intellectually and humanly*, thus developing one's personality. Such enrichment is not measured by the quantity of one's reading and by the extent of one's knowledge, but by the quality of *personal assimilation* and deepening of what one knows.

7.12 *Informative reading* requires that one reads "*multa, sed non multum*", many things but not too accurately, and without taking too much trouble to assimilate. Concretely:
— The *general means of information*, e.g. encyclopedias,

manuals (cf. above 2.1; 5.3; 5.4) must be *consulted assiduously*, without however giving too much time to a detailed reading.

— Similarly, one must take *rapid note* of many books, making a good study of their Table of Contents and reading some pages (e.g. the Introduction or the Conclusion and that chapter which touches the precise point which is of interest to one), with the purpose of finding out what the book is really speaking about and what kind of book it is (popular, scientific, very analytic, offering a new synthesis, etc.). From the results of this rapid inquiry one then makes a *brief note*, so that one can later get back to the book if needed. (One who is well abreast of some discipline could also form a good idea of a book by looking at the bibliography and notes.)

— *Skimming through a book is instead useless*, because one's attention is caught only those few assertions that are already known, which one then mentally orders according to one's own ideas. Therefore "to skim through a book is to find there what one already knows" (M. Blondel). Sometimes of course, in the absence of a good Table of Contents, one has no other option but to skim through the book in order to find the few pages which are really worth reading.

— *To be regularly read* are some *general cultural review* and, if one has a specialization, one or two reviews most representative of that specialization. This enables one to follow the "general movement of ideas" and to keep oneself up-to-date regarding the more important new publications.

7.13 *Formative reading* instead follows the old principle: *"Non multa, sed multum"*, that is, a very intense reading, with slow and deep assimilation, of *few and selected* works which are to be read even *repeatedly*. The following is a list of such works, in order of decreasing importance:

— The *sources* in a broad sense, i.e. not only those listed above (5.2) but also the works of the great philosophers or theologians of the past.

— The *classical monographs*, i.e. those works *on* the

sources (secondary literature) which are always referred to and cited, because they constitute important and sometimes definitive steps in the interpretation of the sources and in the elaboration of a synthesis (e.g. B. LONERGAN, *Insight;* K. RAHNER, *Hörer des Wortes;* etc.). One may obtain an index of the importance of these 'classical' works from the number of their re-editions and translations.

— The *most recent and/or specialized* book or article on the question which one is studying, because this presents the most recent state of research, and saves much other reading, embracing also the results of previous studies.

7.14 *The order in which one reads* on a particular theme is normally the following: first some *reference work*, in order to orient oneself in a broad way on the question in hand; then one or other of the *principal sources* (at least a first orientative reading); and *only at the end* some *monograph*, to enlarge one's horizon of interpretation, confronting it with others.

NB: One must be rather *sober* in reading *monographs* in order not to waste time uselessly. In fact, most of the books and articles, even scientific ones, are not published for their great value, but for economic reasons on the part of the publishers, or for reasons of career on the part of the author. And one must not forget that "the most recent article" in a subject will no longer be the most recent half a year later ...

7.2 How should one read?

For formative reading, the same rules apply, *mutatis mutandis,* as for courses (1.1 above).

7.21 *Read actively.* It is not enough to pick up some 'impressions' from the book; one must instead *reconstruct* for oneself what the author is saying, re-eliciting in one's own mind the ideas that the author had in his. For this, one must:

7.211 *Read with a certain 'preconception'*, i.e. with some idea of what the book is dealing about and how it proceeds, in such a way that one *expects* from the reading an *answer* to definite questions. To this end, one must first study the Table of Contents (2.21 and 7.12 above).

7.212 *Follow the order* of the book itself, because only in this way will one follow the argument of the author. Sometimes, it is true, one must *go ahead without having understood everything*, because certain passages become clear only in the light of what will be said later in the book; one can then return to what was unclear.

7.213 *Read slowly and attentively*, i.e. with a rhythm that allows one to follow the argument thoughtfully. "When one reads too fast or too slowly one follows nothing" (Pascal). Every now and then there is needed a brief pause to recapitulate the argument.

7.214 *Read dialoguing with the author*, as with the professor during the lectures (1.22 above), i.e. taking his affirmations on the one hand with a certain critical reserve, and on the other hand *allowing one's own preconceptions to be modified and corrected* by the reading.

7.22 *Write while reading*, taking note of what one has understood during the reading, as well as of the reflections that occur while reading. Therefore, while reading, one must *always have at hand paper and pencil or pen*, so that one can construct a "materialized memory" of the fruits of the reading. *Four types of notes* can be made:

7.221 *Notes in the margin of the book*, as in the textbook (cf. above 2.22), but obviously this can be done only when the book is one's own, and *never in those borrowed from the library* or from others!! In a second (or third) reading of the book one can then refer directly to the passages marked as important. In books borrowed for a sufficient length of time, the most important passages can be marked with a *bookmark*, and later notes can be made.

7.222 *A specialized index* of points which are of particular interest, noting down on a large paper the names or notions which have to do with the problem one is dealing with (in the written work or dissertation), together with the page references. At the end one could compile an alphabetical index (if useful) simply by cutting the paper and arranging the items in alphabetical order.

7.223 *A continuous summary* of the whole book or of some chapter, on large size pages (or notebook), somewhat like the notes taken in class (above 1.242). This is *not a question of copying* or even abbreviating whole passages of the book, but of writing down *what one has understood* of what the author is saying. Such a summary allows one to recapitulate the whole book rapidly, and can constitute ready material for a "report" or for the "summary" part of a written work, or even for certain chapters of a "dissertation" (cf. below 8 and 9).

7.224 *Notes on cards* for *conserving* information, ideas, formulations or one's own reflections which seem particularly relevant, whether for the work in hand or for any other future use (e.g. catechesis, courses to be given, etc.). While the other three types of annotations are a help and an extension of my understanding of what I read, the notes on cards *conserve the material* for future use, perhaps in a manner which has little to do with the present reading of the book. The advantage of cards is that, since *each one contains only a single point*, they can be ordered and *regrouped* as one likes.

NB 1: Operations 7.222 - 7.224 can now be done directly on a computer — provided that the *work on the computer does not substitute for attentive (and "meditative") reading!* Cf. below 11.23.

NB 2: Obviously, the annotations on the book (7.221) or the compiling of an index (7.222) can be done only if the book is one's own or if it is easily accessible in the library. For books which are more difficult to obtain, one must make summaries and/or annotations on schede (7.223 and 7.224) in a *more complete manner*, such that they can substitute for a reconsultation of the book. One can even make photocopies of some important pages (after having read them!), annotating them later as described in 7.221.

7.3 *Making and using notes on file cards*

7.31 *Materially,* the schede on which one takes notes should be of a *uniform size* (the most convenient: the "postcard" size: 105 x 148 mm), and the *paper should not be too thin* (but it is not necessary and not even convenient that they be of cardpaper). Whether they are lined or marked etc. is not really important: that is a pure luxury. The cards are normally used horizontally, but if one wants to write summaries on cards, one could also write vertically. Whatever the case, one should always leave sufficient space at the top of the cards for the classification headings.

7.32 *Four types of notes* can be written on cards:

7.321 *Literal citations*, copied from the book, which one wants to preserve in their original formulation, either because *the formulation seems to be particularly apt and pregnant,* or because one foresees that one will have to *cite it literally later on*. Such formulations are usually the *definitions* of terms.

What has been copied literally must *always be included within inverted commas*: "...". One must also always copy down the exact reference; and one must check immediately whether the text has been copied without errors.

Examples:

"Studium *philosophiae* non est ad hoc quod sciatur, quid
homines senserint, sed qualiter se habeat veritas rerum"
                    St. Thomas, In. Cael, 1,22
                                        (nr. 228)

Theology:
   — *Subjective* meaning: "the knowledge which God
      has of himself in his Word, in which he knows
      everything, and which he communicates to human
      beings in revelation"
   — *Objective* meaning: "the science which has God as
      object";
         — "natural" theol.: "reaches God through the
            work of creation and with the light of natur-
            al reason"
         — theol. "properly speaking": "reaches God
            through the word and testimony of God
            about himself and with the light of reason
            illuminated by faith"   ·
         — theol. of "the fatherland": "to know God in
            his essence and with the light of glory"
                    Latourelle, Teologia scienza...
                                        p. 11-14

7.322 *Brief information*, formulated in one's own words,
about what is found in the book, *referring back* to the book
itself. If the book is easily available, such indications can be
very brief; if instead one foresees that the book will not be easily accessible, one needs a *brief but more accurate summary*,
including perhaps some literal quotations, so that one can later
use the scheda without having to depend on the book.

With cards of this type, one could, for example, slowly
constitute a "schedario" of philosophers or of theologians, collecting all that one finds on them.

Example:

Readings in theology — chosen;
reviews recommended:
        cf. Alszeghy - Flick, Come si fa la Teologia
                                pp. 202-203

7.323 *One's own reflections* (or even pregnant *formulations*) which occur during the reading, and, if one is preparing a paper, also *schemes, problems* to be discussed, etc. In order to make the reading of these more useful later on, it may be useful to note down the reference and/or the date on which the note is written. To distinguish these personal reflections from other material, they may be *included within square brackets* [...].

Example:

[Is Huber's definition of "structure" (Critica 12.005) valid also for the "ontological structure" of which Fr. Welten speaks?]

7.324 *Bibliographical information*, as will be described below, 7.423.

7.33 *To preserve and use the cards*, these should first be gathered and *put in order ("classified")*. In order to facilitate this, one must indicate the topic at the time of taking the note itself, and this may be done either by means of a *key-word* at the top of the scheda or else by means of an *underlining* in the text itself. When a certain number of cards has been gathered, one can proceed to their *classification*:

7.331 If the cards are for the preparation of some *written work*, the classification of the cards and the *elaboration of the plan* or scheme of the work (cf. below 8.22; 9.22; 10.31; 11.24) will proceed simultaneously.

7.332 If the cards are to be *preserved for a long time* and for *various uses* (the cards prepared for some particular work can also be re-used in various ways), one needs *a more objective and complete classification*. One should take care however that the classification remain always in some way *"personal"*, e.g. according to the study one has completed or according to one's principal areas of interest.

For the *subdivisions* it may be convenient to follow simply a *historical order* (history of philosophy, of the Councils, etc.) or the order of some *basic book* which one knows almost by heart (Sacred Scripture, the Spiritual Exercises, the Summa Theologica, etc.) and the chapters of which can be easily "associated" with the material gathered.

One could fix the classification according to the scheme of the so-called *"decimal classification"* (where 1-9 are the principal groups, 1.1, 1.2, 1.3, etc. 1.11, 1.12, etc. the subdivisions). One *writes* the corresponding number on the *top right-hand corner* of the card, and one must make sure *to keep a written copy of the scheme of classification*.

7.333 *Materially* the classified cards are *grouped and conserved* in special *boxes* (with subdivisions of colored cardpaper; portable boxes are also available), which facilitate research and cards consultation (even without having to take out the cards). In a simpler way, for smaller quantities of cards (e.g. for a written work) one could simply put together the groups of cards with a *paper-clip* and insert these into *envelopes*, thus ensuring greater mobility.

7.334 *The cards are used* not only for *determinate tasks* (by making use of the material found under various headings), nor even merely as an *aid to the memory* (for verifying citations, searching for bibliographical indications, etc.); one should also take advantage of the treasure thus accumulated, by re-reading, in a moment of leisure, some part of the old cards, in order *to find there new inspiration.*

NB 1: When one goes to work in the library, one should therefore always carry a sufficient quantity of blank cards.

NB 2: The work of making cards could be done directly on the computer, with the advantages and disadvantages which will be indicated below, 11.2.

NB 3: One should avoid putting down on this "materialized memory" all that is not worthy of being conserved. Equally one should avoid "making a collection" of cards (like one collects postage stamps), only for the sake of filling up the different sections of the *card file.*

PRACTICAL EXERCISES: 1. Read some substantial article or chapter of a book and make a summary *while reading.*

2. On the occasion of some other reading, take notes on cards in the way described.

7.4 *Bibliographical research*

For normal purposes it is enough to have the bibliographical indications given in the lectures and in the textbook, supplemented eventually by those found in encyclopedias and manuals; one has only to make a selection. When instead one has to write a *substantial dissertation* on a determinate theme, it is important to know not only what one *can* read, but also what one *must* read, identifying in the vast ocean of publications *those few* which regard exactly *the point in question*, or which demand attention because of their *extraordinary quality*. In order to identify these few works (books or articles), it is necessary to first obtain a *global vision of the material offered*, for which one should proceed ideally as follows:

7.41 *First get acquainted* briefly with the problem which one undertakes to deepen in the readings, so as to be able to *ori-*

entate oneself right from the beginning. Usually one will already have obtained such an orientation from the lectures and/or from personal study; if not, one could read some articles from the *Encyclopedias* (cf. above 5.3), or the relevant chapter from some *Manual* or *Compendium of history,* etc.

7.42 *Gather a complete bibliography* on the chosen theme, with the help of the following tools:

7.421 *For philosophy:*

Bibliographical introductions, which indicate the existing bibliographies for every field of research:

H.J. KOREN, *Research in Philosophy. A bibliographical introduction to philosophy and a few suggestions for dissertations.* Pittsburgh-Louvain, Duquesne Univ.-Nauwelaerts, 1966.

R.T. DE GEORGE, *A Guide to Philosophical Bibliography and Research.* New York, Appleton, 1971. [The most complete collection of bibliographical tools and works of consultation in philosophy.]

H. GUERRY, *A Bibliography of Philosophical Bibliographies.* Westport CA, Greenwood, 1977.

G. SCHWINGE, *Bibliographische Nachschlagewerke sur Theologie und ihren Grenzgebieten. Systematisch geordenete Auswahl.* München, Verlag Dokumentation, 1975 [A bibliographical tool not only for philosophy and theology but also for history of religions, pedagogy, etc.]

W. TOTOK, *Bibliographischer Wegweiser der philosophischen Literatur.* Frankfurt, Klostermann, [2]1985. [Indicates the more important bibliographical tools.]

Thematic bibliographies, ordered systematically or historically:

G. VARET, *Manuel de bibliographie philosophique,* 2 vols. Paris, PUF, 1956. [vol. I: History of philosophy; vol. II: Systematic philosophy.]

G.F. McLEAN, *A Bibliography of Christian Philosophy and Contemporary Issues.* New York, Ungar, 1967. [Systematic.]

S.A. MATCZAK, *Philosophy. A Select, Classified Bibliography of Ethics, Economics, Law, Politics, Sociology.* Louvain-Paris, Nauwelaerts, 1970.

W. TOTOK, *Handbuch der Geschichte der Philosophie.* 6 vol. Frankfurt, Klostermann, 1964-90. [Composed almost exclusively of bibliographical information.]

For the *history of philosophy,* abundant material may be found also in:

Grande Antologia Filosofica, ed. U. PADOVANI. 31 vol. Milan: Marzorati, 1954-78.

Questioni di storiografia filosofica, ed. V. MATHIEU - A. BAUSOLA. 6 vol. Brescia, La Scuola, 1974-78.

Besides, there are special bibliographies for many authors, and also some national philosophical bibliographies.

Current bibliographies which are almost exhaustive:

For the years 1934-1945 see:

G.A. DE BRIE, *Bibliographia philosophica 1934-1945.* 2 vol. Maastricht-Brussel, Spectrum, 1960. [vol. I: History of philosophy; vol. II: Systematic philosophy; book-reviews are also indicated after each title.]

For the subsequent years:

Répertoire bibliographique de la philosophie. (Up to 1940, this is part of *Revue Néoscholastique de Philosophie = Revue Philosophique de Louvain*). Louvain, Institut Supérieur de Philosophie, 1924- [Four issues a year, the last of which contains the indices and the list of book-reviews.]

7.422 *For theology*:

Besides the already cited SCHWINGE (7.42), a bibliography of theological bibliographies may be found in:

M. CHAPPIN, *Strumenti di lavoro per la teologia*. Roma, PUG, 1990, pp. 9-15.

General thematic bibliographies:

F.W. BAUTZ, *Biographisch-Bibliographisches Kirchenlexikon*. 2 volumes to date. Hamm, T. Bautz, 1975-
[Useful especially for the bibliographies, which are listed only for authors who are already dead].
J.G. HEINTZ, *Bibliographie des sciences théologiques*. Paris, PUF, 1972 [easy to consult, Protestant].
J.F. MITROS, *Religions. A. Select, Classified Bibliography*. Louvain-Paris, Nauwelaerts, 1973 [Christian religion, pp. 195-399].
R.P. MORRIS, *A Theological Book List*, produced by the Theological Education Fund, New York-Oxford, Blackwell, 1960.
Completed by:
A.M. WARD, alii, *A Theological Book List*. English Supplement 1 and 2, *ibid.*, 1963, 1968.
Sociologia de la religión y teología. Estudio bibliografico. 2 vol. Madrid, Editorial Cuadernos para el Diálogo, 1975-78.
Das evangelische Schrifttum. Gesamtausgabe 1979. 2 vol. Stuttgart, Vereinigung evangelischer Buchhändler, 1979.
Das katholische Schrifttum. Gesamtausgabe 1979. Stuttgart, Verband katholischer Verleger und Buchhändler. 1979 [systematic list of all theological books in German which are actually available].

Specialized bibliographies for certain areas of theology:

G.S. GLANZMAN – J.A. FITZMYER, *An Introductory Bibliography for the Study of Scripture*. Westminster, Newman, 1961.
S.B. MARROW, *Basic Tools of Biblical Exegesis*. A student's manual. Roma, P.I. Biblico, 1976.
P.E. LANGEVIN, *Bibliographie biblique 1930-1983*. 3 vol. Québec, Univ. Laval, 1972-78.
E. MALATESTA, *St. John's Gospel 1920-1965*. Roma, P.I. Biblico, 1967.

A.J. MATTILL – M.B. MATTILL, *A Classified Bibliography of Literature on the Acts of the Apostles*. Leiden, Brill, 1966.

A. METZGER, *Index to Periodical Literature on the Apostle Paul*. Leiden, Brill, 1961.

B. METZGER, *Index to Periodical Literature on Christ and the Gospels*. Leiden, Brill, 1966.

A. VAN ROEY – G. DEESEN, *Bibliographia Patristica*. Patres latini 1900-1914. Leuven, Keizersberg, 1974 [will be continued till 1955, where the bibliography of SCHNEEMELCHER begins].

U. VALESKE, *Votum Ecclesiae. II Teil. Interkonfessionelle ekklesiologische Bibliographie*. München, Claudius, 1962.

N. HEINRICHS, *Bibliographie der Hermeneutik und ihrer Andwendung seit Schleiermacher*. Düsseldorf, Philosophia, ²1972.

Current bibliographies, general and specialized:

Ephemerides Theologicae Lovanienses. Elenchus Bibliographicus. Louvain, Univ. Catholica Lovaniensis 1924- [the best, and in fact the only current bibliography that is almost complete and that covers all the areas of theology].

The Catholic Periodical and Literature Index. A cumulative author and subject index to a selected list of catholic periodicals. Howerford, PA, Catholic Library Association, 1939- [not very complete; but contains also an index of book reviews].

Theologische Revue. Theologische Bibliographie. Auswahl von neuerschienen Büchern und Aufsätzen zur Theologie und ihrer Grenzgebiete. Münster, Aschendorff, 1954- [6 fascicles per year, easy to consult].

Bibliografía teológica commentada del area iberoamericana. Buenos Aires, Istituto Superior Evangelico de Estudios Teologicos, 1973- [Covers also "Ciencias sociales" and "Filosofía"].

Répertoire biblique des Institutions Chrétiennes (RIC). Index en cinq langues établi par ordinateur. Strasbourg, CERDIC, 1967-

P. NOBER, *Elenchus bibliographicus biblicus*. [up to 1963, united with: *Biblica*]; from 1988: *Elenchus of Biblica*. Roma, P.I. Biblico, 1920- [exhaustive information].

W. SCHNEEMELCHER, *Bibliographia Patristica*. International Patristic Bibliography. To date, vol. XIII (1968). Berlin, Gruyter, 1959-

P. ARATO, *Bibliographia Historiae Pontificiae*, in: *Archivum Historiae Pontificiae*. Roma, P.U. Gregoriana, 1963- [precious for the documents of the Magisterium].

G.M. BESUTTI, *Bibliografia Mariana 1950-* 7 volumes to date. Roma, Marianum, 1952-

Inernationale ökumenische Bibliographie. Mainz, Grünewald, 1967-

7.423 From these bibliographies, one notes down on *bibliographical cards* the titles of those books and articles which *could possibly* be of interest. Cards meant for bibliography should be different either in color or in size (e.g. 7.5 x 10 cm) from the other cards (described above 7.31). They should contain:

For books:

Name of author (Initials + Surname)
Title of book. Subtitle, which gives a more complete indication of what the book is about.
the volume number if any
number of pages.
Place, Publisher, edition, year.

Example:

M. Blondel,
L'Action (1893). Essai d'une critique de la vie et d'une science de la pratique.
XXV-495 pp.
Paris, PUF, [3]1973.

For articles:

Name of author.
Complete title of article.
in: Review, volume (year).
from page ... to page

Example:

J. Alfaro,
El tema bíblico en la enseñanza de la teología sistemática.
in: Gregorianum 50 (1969).

507-541

The same information (omitting only the number of pages in a book) can be included in the *bibliography of some written work*; the only difference is that they will be written in a continuous line.

NB: For works which are exclusively bibliographical, the bibliographical card must contain also:
1. The complete first name, so as to avoid confusion between, for example, P(ietro) and P(aolo) Rossi. In such a case, the first name is written *after* the surname.
2. Information about the series in which the book is published, with the series number. This is written in brackets after the subtitle.
3. The complete name of the publisher (e.g. "Sheed & Ward" and not merely "Sheed").

For any further doubts, one may consult:

L.M. MARTÍNEZ-FAZIO, *Paradigmata quaedam citationum bibliographicarum.* Rome, PUG, ^{2}1977.
J. JANSSENS, *Note di metodologia.* Parte prima. Rome, PUG, 1988, p. 9-41.

NB: To make the bibliographical cards complete and more useful, *one could add*: — on the top right-hand corner, the Call Number in the library (if one always works in the same library); — brief remarks about the content of the book or article (cf. below 7.4.3 for hints about how to do this), and also information about book-reviews.

7.43 *Determine the importance and the contents* of the books which seem relevant to the theme chosen. So as not to waste time in reading books or articles which are not really important and even out-of-date or irrelevant, it is useful *to form a preliminary judgment* about the scientific value of the book in question: whether it really deals with the theme; whether it contributes something new; whether it is a serious book. Such a judgment can be formed, even without actually having the book in hand, with the following *tools:*

7.431 *For philosophy:*

Annotated bibliographies (which give not only the titles in systematic order, but also a brief note about each):

G.F. McLEAN, *An Annotated Bibliography of Philosophy in Catholic Thought 1900-1964.* New York, Ungar, 1967.
Bibliography philosophique. I. Bibliographie d'histoire de la philosophie 1945-65 (Bibliographie française établie à l'intention des lecteurs étrangers). Paris, A.D.P.F., s.d. [Only French books].

Current bibliographies with "abstracts" (or brief summaries of the content of books or articles listed):

Bibliographie de philosophie. Bibliography of Philosophy. Paris, Institut International de Philosophie, 1937- [Analyzes only books].
Bulletin signalétique [up to 1968]: 19 Philosophie et sciences religieuses; [from 1969]: 519 Philosophie, 527 Sciences Religieuses. Paris, Centre de Documentation de Sciences Humaines, 1940- [Was analyzing only articles; the indications are very brief and not always accurate; is now suspended].
The Philosophers Index. An International Index to Philosophical Periodicals. Bowling Green, Philosophy Documentation Center, 1967- [Analyses articles and contributions to "collections"; the summaries are by the authors themselves].

A list of *book reviews* may be found in: DE BRIE, G.A.,

Répertoire bibliographique (above 7.421) and *The Philosophers Index.* To get a good idea of a book one must read (at least) *two* reviews in journals of different tendencies.

7.432 *For theology*, the means of information are more specialized; besides the already mentioned *Bulletin signalétique* we may note:

Internationale Zeitschriftenschau für Bibelwissenschaft und Grenzgebiete. International Review of Biblical Studies. Düsseldorf, Patmos, 1951-

New Testament Abstract. A record of current periodical literature. Cambridge MA, Weston College, 1956- [in recent years, reviews also books].

Old Testament Abstracts. Washington, Catholic University, 1978- [reviews articles and books].

Religion Index One: Periodicals (earlier: *Index to Religious Periodical Literature*). Chicago, American Theological Library Association, 1949- [gives summaries from 1975 onwards].

Religious and Theological Abstracts. Myerstown PA, 1958-

Bulletin de Théologie ancienne et médiévale. Louvain, Mont César, 1929- [up to 1970, 2 fascicles per year; then one; very reliable, but considerably delayed].

Rassegna di letteratura tomistica [continuation of *Bulletin thomiste 1924-1965*]. Napoli, Domenicane, 1969 [philosophy and theology, from the Thomist point of view].

Medioevo latino. Bollettino bibliografico della cultura europea dal secolo VI al XIII. Spoleto, Centro Italiano di Studi sull'Alto Medio Evo, 1980-

For keeping abreast of the current publications in a given discipline, the regular 'Bulletins' (2-4 per fascicle) on theology as well as on philosophy, in the following periodical are very useful:

Revue des Sciences philosophiques et théologiques. Paris, Vrin, 1921-

An index of the *reviews* of books may be found in *Catholic Periodical and Literature Index.*

PRACTICAL EXERCISE: Prepare some bibliographical

cards on some particular author or problem: one "classic", one more recent book and article. Indicate also the reviews of the book.

8. The Written Report and the Thematic Elaboration

However active and formative one's reading may be, it is not an end in itself, nor is it merely for one's own cultural formation. One reads above all in order to be able to give *something of one's own* to others. The receptive phase of creative study is wholly geared to the productive phase.

Such a "product" of one's study will always be, in one way or other, *something written*, because even for an oral report (in a seminar), for lectures or for a conference one needs at least a written scheme; therefore we will speak here only of written works. According to the level of personalization we can distinguish *three types* of such written works:

— The *report* simply "reports" what someone else has written, adding at the most a few personal criticisms or observations. Nevertheless even a report constitutes a work that is *authentically creative*: it is a question in fact of re-creating, of making an argument, a thought, or a controversy alive once again. The contributions of individuals at a seminar will normally be in the form of reports; at the scientific level the report develops into a *critical review or in a "bulletin"* (critical and comparative review of several books or articles on the same theme).

— The *thematic elaboration* is a question of material collected from different authors regarding a particular theme and in view of that theme. But if the material comes mainly from others, the *organization of the material belongs to the one who is writing*. In this category are included, besides *scholastic exercises* which normally fall in the category of "thematic elaborations", also *"popularizing"* books and articles, manuals and *textbooks*, and also many other publications which, though claiming to be scientific, are really only compilations.

— The *dissertation* instcad is an *original work* of the one writing: the results of historical research, a new interpretation of the sources, a new synthesis, etc. Such a work is of course based on the readings done; still, it can hold its own and remains the exclusive responsibility of its author, who nonetheless must ensure that his assertions are based on *sufficient evidence*. The *doctoral thesis* must be of this type (and also, in a lesser way, the *Master's thesis*), as also *every book and article that is truly scientific*.

8.1 *How to write a report*

8.11 *The material* for the report is the book (or article or chapter) itself which is assigned for reporting, and *nothing else*. A first gathering of the material is done in the *summary made while reading* (above 7.223). It is not enough however to simply reproduce such a summary, or to repeat the book: "The author says...; then he says ...; at the end he says..."; one must *read the text several times* (making use also of commentaries and interpretations), so as to *identify clearly*: the *thesis* of the author; *why* he proposes this thesis and in these terms; how he *demonstrates* and develops his thesis. In other words: one must first grasp the *substance* of the text in question; only then will one be able to add some nuances and details.

8.12 *The work of redaction* will consist precisely in *presenting clearly*, for the benefit of the readers (and more so if there are merely "listeners"), the substance of the text, making evident the interconnections of the various assertions (omitting those which are less important, or merely mentioning them briefly). Therefore before writing, one must so to say *"reconstruct" in one's mind* the text which one will be presenting. In the actual exposition of this reconstruction however, one will normally follow the *order of exposition of the author himself* (and if, for reasons of clarity, one must change this order, one must say so explicitly).

8.13 *For the external presentation* of the report the following rules must be followed:

8.131 Although the report must be *concise,* one must be careful not to be too elliptical, mentioning only the principal points.

8.132 One may give *literal citations* of one or two of the more revealing and characteristic expressions or assertions of the author; one must however avoid presenting a report which is a pure "mosaic of citations".

8.133 Since a report is usually rather brief, the structure is *not* normally highlighted by means of *subtitles*; instead, *paragraphs* are clearly distinguished. This must be done according to the criteria of logic, not of graphics! When the report consists of parts which are quite different, these may be *numbered.* For the benefit of the students, it is useful to begin the report with a *scheme.*

8.134 *A second redaction* is normally necessary to bring the report to perfection. This is done on the basis of the first redaction, checking and improving the *fidelity*, *clarity* and conciseness.

NB: A *critical (scientific) book review* consists substantially of a report of this type, preceded by: the exact *bibliographical information* regarding the book being reviewed (supplied according to the norms of the journal in which the review will be published), and a very brief overview of the book. One concludes by adding observations and *critical discussions*, and also an *overall appreciation.*
Since the scientific value of a book review lies in the critical observations, Such observations can be made only by one who is *at least as expert* in the matter as the author of the book being reviewed. One who lacks such competence should limit himself to writing a *bibliographical notice.*

PRACTICAL EXERCISE: write a brief report (of one or two pages) of an article or chapter of a book (these could be the same as in the previous exercise), and discuss it.

8.2 *How to prepare a Thematic Elaboration*

8.21 *Gathering the material.* Besides some orientative reading (manuals, encyclopedias), one must read *three or four of the more important books or articles* on the theme (either "classics", or the more specialized, or the most recent), as far as possible of *different tendencies* and types (some more panoramic, some more analytic). It is not necessary to read the whole of each book, but only enough to understand well its character, and the chapter or *chapters directly pertinent to the theme.*

The material obtained from these readings is collected on *cards*; if one is in a position to retain the books while one is working on the elaboration, it would be useful to mark the more important passages with *bookmarks,* so that they can be easily found when needed.

8.22 *The organization of the material* is done in function both of the material gathered as well as of the theme. Having finished the readings and made cards from the books and articles, one *re-reads all the cards* "meditatively", *putting together* (remember the paper-clip!) those which deal with the same aspect of the theme. Having thus identified and made clear (almost mechanically) certain aspects of the theme, one begins to *reflect:* which among these aspects is the *principal* one (i.e. which responds exactly to the question posed or clarifies best the theme adopted)? Which of the other aspects are *presuppositions,* which are *consequences* of the principal answer? Is there material (i.e. aspects) which can simply be ignored? Is there perhaps some fundamental obscurity which calls for further research? As a result of these reflections one establishes a *first tentative plan.*

8.221 *The plan* of an elaboration (and of any other written work) must:

— *proceed logically* (beginning with those things which are necessary to understand the others, and avoiding leaps from one theme to another);

— *be clear and evident* (in such a way that the logical progression is manifest even from a mere reading of the plan; to facilitate such clarity it is very useful to give concise and pregnant "titles" to each point);

— *be complete* (neither omitting nor hiding in some subdivision any important aspect of the problem).

8.222 *The individual points* of the plan must then be reconsidered one by one, re-reading all the material which is referred to. Doing this, one tries to identify:

— *where the authors read agree:* if the agreement is unanimous, one can consider the point as established;

— *where their interpretations or syntheses are in conflict:* here one tries to form a personal judgment on the bearing of the disagreement and on the more probable opinion (that is, that which is supported by better arguments);

— *what still remains obscure* or disputable in the individual points, searching, as far as possible, for further clarifications (by reconsulting the books already read or even by reading some other book).

8.23 *The redaction* begins only after this "reflective" phase and on the basis of a *second plan which has been completed and adjusted.* Drawing up the elaboration is not in fact a simple matter of reproducing the material accumulated in an order that is more or less coherent, but of *saying in one's own words what one has understood* while organizing the material. References to authors read are made only for *supporting, justifying and illustrating* this understanding. Here also therefore one must *avoid the "mosaic of citations"* (a temptation which is all the stronger when one has on one's desk, or better still in the computer, a mass of cards, all of them "precious"!).

Regarded as a whole, the *written text* of an elaboration (or of a conference, lecture, etc.) must contain the following *four moments*:

"— *An interesting entry* into the material, which arouses curiosity; clear, beginning from notions quite familiar to the reader; brief, without digressions which tire and divide the attention, but leading quickly to the point to be discussed.

— *State well the question* to be discussed (at times, following St. Thomas, in the form of *Videtur quod non*); with precision, explaining new or rare terms, distinguishing the point to be studied from related questions.

— *Develop* the argument from the known to the unknown, with transitions which are easy for the mind; avoid jumping from one argument to another, but deal with every argument completely before going on to another; divide the matter not according to an abstract a priori plan, but in such a way as to present the *real* problems, the points that are really necessary or useful to explain.

— *Conclude* clearly, exactly and neatly, distinguishing what seems to have been established and what remains doubtful"[1].

8.24 *The external presentation* of an elaboration comprises, besides the text itself well subdivided by means of *subtitles* (but not too many!): (1) a *cover page* (with the name of the author and the title, indicating also the course or the professor for whom the elaboration is done, as also one's registration number); (2) the *plan* of the elaboration (not necessarily in the form of a table of contents with page references) and, above all, (3) the *bibliography* of books and articles used by the author. The *footnotes* serve only to identify the citations (which must be few but substantial).

PRACTICAL EXERCISE: compose an elaboration according to the indications of a professor and discuss it during the various phases of its composition: the plan, the redaction, the external presentation.

---

[1] J. DE GUIBERT, in: *Il metodo dello studio*. Rome, PUG, 1928, p. 28-29.

8.3 *While writing, always pay attention to:*

8.31 *The 'audience' to whom the work is addressed.* Like one who speaks, one who writes also wants *to say something to someone* — which can range from wanting to demonstrate one's ability to a professor up to the proclamation of the gospel to the people of our time. Therefore it is important to keep in mind, in the first place, the *situation of the one being addressed*: who is he? what does he know already? what does he expect from my writing? what do I find useful or necessary to communicate to him? how can I provoke his interest?

8.32 *The difference between the order of discovery and the order of exposition.* It is neither necessary nor useful to lead the reader along the path by which one arrived at the results of one's research. Perhaps one arrived at the "key point" which clarified everything only at the end of the research; but this point must be presented to the reader at the very beginning. The same can be said, for example, about the hidden presuppositions of the author being interpreted, which are often discovered only at the end of a long research.

8.33 *The appropriateness of the language and style* to the subject which is being discussed. In a scientific work, the language and style must be *clear and sober.* "As regards language: correctness, purity, exactness in the choice of words (in the use of synonyms); also, richness of vocabulary. As regards style: incisiveness and sobriety, cutting down useless words, excessive adjectives and superlatives; — personality, avoiding stereotyped phrases, easy and common formulae, making an effort to speak about the things in hand, adapting the style perfectly to express them; — sensible modernity, neither the style of yesterday not that of tomorrow, but that of today, which facilitates reading today"[2]. In order to attain such *incisiveness and con-*

---

[2] J. DE GUIBERT, *op. cit.,* p. 27.

ciseness of language, the first thing that is needed is *clarity in ideas* ("Rem tene, verba sequentur", or else with Boileau: "What is well conceived is clearly expressed, And the words to say it arrive easily"); in this sense the ability to express is a wonderful way of finding out whether one has really understood. Again, the use of a well-chosen (and coherent) *metaphor* or image, as well as the insertion of some concrete example, is not at all a bad idea for philosophical or theological writing. However, a pompous or florid style should be avoided.

The capacity to write well comes only as the result of continuous *exercises in style*. One must habituate oneself to *write regularly* ("nulla dies sine linea"!) and to write *with care,* rereading and *correcting* one's writing.

The following books contain useful advice for the redaction of scientific works:

J. BRUN, and others, *L'art de composer et de rédiger.* Amiens-Bruxelles, Éd. scientifiques-Baud, 1963.
K.L. TURABIAN, *A Manual for Writers of Term Papers, Theses and Dissertations.* Chicago, Univ. of Chicago, [25]1987.

Cf. also the practical books of style in the various languages.

9. The Master's Dissertation

While the elaboration and redaction of reports and thematic elaborations are based upon the material given, the preparation of a dissertation proceeds in the opposite way: one *begins from a problem*, and in function of this problem one proceeds to *search for bibliographical material*. That is why the formulation of the theme itself is of decisive importance for the success of a research which should result in a dissertation.

9.1 *The choice of theme*

At the graduate level, the theme must always be chosen

according to the advice of the professor, because only he has the global vision necessary for judging the feasibility of the dissertation. Besides, the theme should always be one that can be developed by means of a *recourse to and interpretation of certain definite texts.*

9.11 *The theme must be proportionate* both to the facilities (libraries) and to the time available, as well as to the capacity (knowledge of languages, etc.) and interests of the student (personal preferences, future work, etc.). In this connection it is useful to note that a theme, which at first sight appears very "existential", often brings less satisfaction in its working out than some other, more "objective" but more precise theme, which constrains one to adapt oneself to it in the research, thus opening up one's horizon of perception.

9.12 *The choice of theme must be made as early as possible,* so as to give a definite orientation to the research, even to the exploratory research (consultation of encyclopedias and manuals, gathering of bibliography), and so as to avoid wasting time with useless reading.

9.13 *It will often be necessary to restrict the theme,* in the process of the research itself, both materially (texts to be read) as well as formally (aspects to be considered). Only thus can one deal accurately and deeply with the point that is really of interest — and finish one's work within the allotted time.

9.2 *The elaboration of the theme*

9.21 *The preparatory work,* that is the preliminary information, the bibliographical research, the reading and the making of cards, the ordering of the cards, all this is done *in the same way as for the thematic elaboration* (cf. 8.21 and 7.4 above), with the one (but essential) difference that this research be continually *guided and conditioned by the problem* which one intends to clarify. This means that one should not be content with what one "finds" in some particular work; rather, one must *go actively in search of* that book, of that text which casts the desired light on the problem, making a *continuous* effort to *clarify* what still remains obscure and to fill up the lacunae.

9.22 *The work of reflection* constitutes, for this reason, the spine of the research. One must:

9.221 *Analyze* the most important texts, with the *methods of interpretation* learnt in the seminars and courses;

9.222 *Search for a synthesis* of the results of such analysis, not so much "constructing" it as discovering gradually the unity manifested by the results themselves. In fact, if these do not come together in an almost spontaneous manner, one can be quite sure that one has not yet discovered the solution, because "ens = verum = unum". In this search for the synthesis lies the whole value (and the difficulty) in the elaboration of a dissertation.

NB: For *initiating* such a work of speculation or for liberating it when it is grounded, it may be useful to make a sort of *private brainstorming* (cf. 3.22 above), noting on cards, in a moment of leisure and of relaxation, all the ideas which come to mind about the theme.

9.23 *The redaction* of the synthesis obtained itself constitutes its final verification, and must therefore proceed by *concentric steps* and in such a way that the manuscript *lends itself easily to modifications*:

9.231 *A first draft* rapidly fixes the overall development of the theme and the principal passages of the argument. Such a draft can be either a *"concentrate"* of the dissertation consisting of a few well worked out pages, or else a *more detailed plan*.

NB: At least at this point one must *meet the Director* of the dissertation, to check the validity of the prospective results.

9.232 *A first redaction* elaborates extensively at least the *central and decisive parts* of the dissertation. This must be such that corrections and even radical rearrangements are easy to carry out: writing that is well spread out, with large margins, papers *written only on one side* (so as to be able to change the order and even to cut and paste) — unless one is writing on the computer, which makes rearrangements of the text far easier. This first redaction is corrected and re-elaborated until the progression of the argument becomes sufficiently clear.

9.233 *The definitive redaction* adds to the first redaction also the *secondary parts* omitted up to now, like the Introduction, Conclusion, certain precisions or complements, etc. In writing this final redaction, one must be attentive above all to the *linguistic and stylistic form* of the text; it will often be possible to *condense* what was still too diffuse in the first redaction.

9.3 *The presentation of the typescript*

9.31 *The structure of the typescript* as a whole is like that of a printed book: cover page, table of contents, bibliography (the last two may be placed either at the beginning of the dissertation in that order, or at the end, in reverse order: bibliography, table of contents), introduction, the body of the text with footnotes, conclusion.

9.32 *The quotations* should not be too many and must above all be *functional:* they serve either to prove an assertion or because of their pregnant formulation. *Brief citations* (one or a few words up to one or two propositions) are situated *in the text itself within inverted commas*: "...", and *always in the language of the dissertation* (except if it is a question of a technical term). *Longer citations are presented indented* and with reduced line spacing. These could even be given in their original language (provided this is among those which are better known), if this seems important from the point of view of their probatory force. Normally it is better to give them in the language of the dissertation, supplying the original text in the note.

The *sources of the citations must always be indicated*: in *parentheses* in the text itself, if the page reference alone (and perhaps an abbreviated reference to the source) is sufficient; normally however in a *footnote*. One should avoid the indications: *l.c.* (= loco citato) and *op. cit.* (= opus citatum), unless it is a question of referring to an *immediately preceding* indication; otherwise these references remain too vague.

NB: The *American style* of citing the sources within brackets in the text itself, indicating only the author, the year of publication and the page (Henrici, 1992, 87) may be okay for smaller works (articles) with a restricted bibliography.

9.33 *The footnotes* must be put down together with the text itself. Besides the sources of the citations, these notes may contain: references to other parallel or complementary texts, to discussions regarding the point being dealt with, and maybe brief allusions to other problems connected to the point being discussed. *They should never contain something that is more important that the text* (something that puts the principal text in question, or else something that is indispensable for understanding the principal text). On the whole, one should be rather *sober in putting* notes; more substantial but collateral discussions (e.g. a detailed discussion about a secondary point) may also be placed in an *Appendix*.

PART FIVE

INITIATION TO RESEARCH

The goal of every disciple is to become a teacher one day, just as sons eventually become fathers. Being a master presupposes the ability to transmit to others what one has learned and continues to learn. Such a capacity should be acquired through the study for the Master's degree ("licentiate"), which confers the "licence to teach". But to be a master signifies something much more: the ability to teach something of one's own, the results of one's own research. The study for the doctorate is therefore essentially an initiation to research, not so much for learning particular techniques of research, as for planning, bringing to completion and publishing one's own, original research in the doctoral thesis. This normally calls for two or three full years of hard, solitary work of research and redaction, for which we would like to offer some very general counsels.

In many ways, becoming a master is more difficult and arduous than becoming a parent. Not everyone succeeds, and it is not even advisable that everyone should try. The pages that follow try to describe this process in some way.

10. The Doctoral Thesis

The doctoral thesis distinguishes itself from the master's dissertation not only by its size (more than 250 pages, as against the 50-80 pages — and not more! — of the dissertation), but above all by the requirement that it make a *truly new contribution to research*, while the dissertation remains, for the most part, a methodological exercise on results that have already been established. The passage to the elaboration of a thesis represents therefore a real qualitative leap, and if it is true that everything that was said in the previous chapter applies also to the doctoral thesis, nonetheless there are also new methodological exigences which are not merely formal.

10.1 *The choice of topic*

The choice of topic is crucial for the success of a thesis, and itself calls for quite some research. It must meet two fundamental criteria, *originality* and *feasibility,* and goes hand in hand with the choice of a director with whom the student feels at ease and who is really competent in the matter chosen.

10.11 *In the ideal case* the professor is able to propose a topic that is already specific and which he has identified as something that calls for research. In this case it is enough for the student to enter into the perspective of the director, and to carry out the preliminary research for determining the state of research, assuring himself of the newness of the theme and of its feasibility. This is an ideal case because the professor will be personally interested in the theme, and will follow the elaboration with greater commitment.

10.12 *In all the other cases*, the theme *takes shape gradually* through a *dialogue*, facilitated by *bibliographical research*, between student and professor. The procedure is from the generic (some particular author or problematic) to the specific, until there has been identified a precise point that lends itself to research, and which is both original and feasible. The choice of the topic must at any rate be done *within a month* (or two at the most) of the start of doctoral work.

In view of the *practical feasibility* of the thesis, the following rules must be followed:

10.121 The theme must always include a *historical or exegetical aspect*, so as to be able to take the support of existing texts and studies, and to use a method of interpretation for at least a part of the thesis. A purely speculative or systematic topic, whether in philosophy or in theology, presupposes a breadth of knowledge and creative thinking which a doctoral student normally does not possess.

The *specific difficulties* presented by the ancient-medieval period as well as by the contemporary period must be taken into account. Theses on antiquity or on the middle ages call for a certain familiarity with historico-critical methods of research and with classical philology, while for contemporary authors or themes, secondary literature is often lacking, as well as that chronological distance which allows a vision of the whole and the possibility of distinguishing the important from the ephemeral. The rule that *one does not write theses on living authors* is therefore opportune.

10.122 The *problematic or particular question* which is to be clarified, or the *hypothesis* which one wants to verify, should be well defined and delimited. The specificity of a "thesis" lies in fact in this: that it be not a work of mere exposition or compilation, but that it contribute *something new* by way of a precise and well-grounded answer to a question that is still open in research on some particular theme or author.

The problematics can be of different types, depending on the interests and capacity of the student: the *correct interpretation* of a text or work, a *thematic research* in one or more authors, a *comparison* of a historical type (dependence) or structural type between various texts or authors, or even a *panoramic research* on the "status quaestionis" in a determinate period or area or in more recent research ("Forschungsbericht"). It must however be noted that though panoramic research at first sight is seemingly easier, in actual fact it usually calls for much more time, work and intelligence. In the same vein, a comparative study should not be attempted except where a historical dependence has already been established or is at least strongly suspected, or else where two authors or texts deal with the same theme in a way that is evidently similar; otherwise the research runs the risk of ending up in a void or in mere guesswork.

10.123 Finally (but also in the first place) the *linguistic competence* of the student must be taken into account. It is true that there are translations; nevertheless, in order to deal with texts from antiquity or from the middle ages there is needed a very good knowledge of Greek and/or Latin. In the same way, the secondary literature for French authors will be principally in French, for German authors in German, etc. Useful as the learning of languages is, normally this should not consume the major part of the time allocated for the doctorate!

NB: The *originality* expected from the results of a thesis forbids that two theses be written contemporaneously on the same theme. Before fixing the topic definitively therefore, the student must make sure that it is *still "free"*, by making a bibliographical research on more recent publications and searching for information on theses in progress (at least in the Roman Universities). For dissertations in German there is a *Deutsche theologische Dissertationenkartei* (cf: JANSSENS, p. 15); for many recent authors, specialized *Archives* are available, which should supply information (and be supplied with information!) on works in progress. For the rest, since philosophy and theology are principally speculative disciplines, studies on the same theme can be repeated at a distance of some years — provided one has something really new to say.

10.13 *The argument must be registered* in the Secretariat as soon as possible; that is to say, when not only the title is sufficiently definite, but also preliminary research has yielded sufficient clarity about the *extent, limits, method*, as well as the expected or desired *results* of the research one wishes to undertake. These four points (but not a detailed plan of the future thesis!) form the content of the *presentation* of the argument, required for its registration.

10.2 *The gathering of material*

The gathering of material distinguishes itself qualitatively from that for a dissertation or other work, in as much as it should be *complete*. Only thus can the thesis insert itself into the actual state of research and contribute something new to it. Since however in many fields absolute completeness is difficult to attain (the literature on an author like Hegel is already extremely vast, and every year there are added more writings than one can read), one must aim at a *sectorial completeness*, keeping in mind the delimitations of the argument (the importance of which one thus begins to see). Practically one proceeds in the manner described below.

10.21 *A rapid orientative survey* using the general means of information (encyclopedias, dictionaries, manuals) gives an overall view of the topic (author and theme) and of its context. Notes are taken of the relevant information as well as of the bibliographical data discovered. It would be useful to read one or two of the *"classical"* monographs (even those not so recent) on the author or theme; these will be found indicated in the encyclopedias and manuals. If possible, the most recent writing/s (if these have already been identified) on the topic must also be read, with the aim of familiarizing oneself with the actual state of research.

10.22 *An extensive bibliographical research*, making use of all the means indicated in 7.42 and 7.43 above, will make one familiar with all that has been published on one's topic. One must take note of: (1) the generic or the *major books* on the author or theme; (2) *everything* (articles, contributions, etc. included) that could possibly be relevant to the *specific* argument. The bibliography thus constituted implies neither that all the writings listed must actually be read, nor that the list will be reproduced as it is in the thesis, nor even that it already contains all the material to be read. It will probably be necessary to carry out further bibliographical research later on, in order to clarify points which still remain obuscure.

The bibliography thus constituted must however be *discussed with the director of the thesis*, with the purpose of identifying both those books which need *not* be read as well as those which are more important.

10.23 With the panoramic vision already acquired, one begins the deeper study of the "text" or "sources" around which the argument is centered; i.e. one reads the author or authors and the works which are more directly pertinent. Applying the rules of active reading (7.2 and 7.3 above), one carries out a reading that is already *accentuated and selective:* besides a general knowledge and understanding of the author and/or of the text, always in their context, those passages which are specially relevant to the argument must be identified and noted down.

Normally a *second reading* will be necessary immediately after the first, because from the knowledge of the whole one understands better the parts. This second reading can be cursory with regard to the less interesting parts, concentrating rather on the parts already noted as relevant. But one should not go on reading "about the author" or "on the theme" endlessly and with little direction; this is really an indication of fear of "attacking" the elaboration of the thesis. Nor should one transcribe entire books or chapters onto cards (or on the computer); instead one should note briefly what is found where.

NB: For some passage that is particularly important or particularly difficult to understand (even linguistically), a good technique may be to write it out *by hand:* re-writing the text thus, together with its author so to say, one "enters" more profoundly into it and into its *ductus.*

10.24 *A first pause for reflection* and for creative relaxation is required after this first phase of reading, or between the first and the second reading of the author. This allows for "digestion" and assimilation of what has been read, re-reading the cards and putting into order one's own thoughts rather than the cards. At this moment there is being formulated, almost spontaneously, a *first hypothesis,* to be verified in the subsequent readings and in the elaboration of the material.

10.25 *The secondary literature,* or the monographs and articles on the author and the theme, are read with greater profit only *towards the end* of this first phase of research. The knowledge of the author and of the problematic that has already been acquired make possible a more *selective* reading, discerning what is useful and illuminating from what is merely superfluous and repetitive. Besides, the interpreters will cast light on *texts and difficulties which have already become familiar* (and which they themselves, in their writing, presuppose as familiar). To put it crudely: it is more profitable (and more creative) to read the interpreters in the light of the text, than to read the text in the light of the interpreters.

As regards the *order* in which to read the secondary literature, there is no fixed rule. It is useful to begin with one of the more recent major monographs; this will easily identify the "classical" monographs, which one can then proceed to read. For the rest it may be more illuminating (and "quicker") to read in an inverse chronological order, beginning from the most recent publications. In this way one can easily see what it is that cannot be ignored in the older publications. Naturally, the rules of active reading continue to be valid (7.2 and 7.3).

10.3 *The thoughtful construction of the 'thesis'*

This is the decisive moment in the elaboration of the thesis, and for this the student must take all the time (and all the *leisure*) necessary. One cannot pass immediately from the collection of the material to the redaction of the thesis; nor is it enough to merely "organize" the material. Since the thesis must give a precise and well-grounded answer to a precise question, it is a question of identifying first of all what *elements of the answer* have been provided by the research and reading undertaken up to now; how these give precision to the very question itself; and what points still remain to be clarified.

10.31 *The organization of the material gathered,* which serves as a preparatory step to reflection, is done as described above for the elaboration and the dissertation (8.22 and 9.21- 9.22). This does not however lead immediately to the elaboration of a plan. It serves instead to:

10.32 *Rethink the results obtained materially.* The cards, even when well organized, do not in fact yield more than what may already be found in print (in the sources and in the secondary literature). Reproducing them would amount at most to an intelligent compilation. It is a question now of drawing out from them new evidence, which will justify the work undertaken. This occurs *in the process of confronting them with the problem* or the precise question which the thesis intends to answer. Thus they will be transformed from information collected into elements of an answer or a solution — elements which, normally, will raise new questions.

It is difficult to describe or to give rules for this work of thinking, one part of which (and perhaps the better part) is done even unconsciously. Still, the Italian words which describe it give (in their Latin etymology) a certain idea.

10.321 *Cogitare* (co-agitare) [English, to cogitate] suggests that the various pieces of information and the elements of thought are "pushed to group themselves". This has already been done in part in the organization of the material; it could be done further on the basis of a brainstorming (9.222 NB above); and it should lead to the bringing together and to the *comparison* of the elements gathered. This will put into evidence certain connections between them, but also contrasts and (at least apparent) contradictions, which will have to be clarified.

10.322 *Pensare* [English, to think] suggests "weighing" [Italian, ponderare] the value and the "weight" [Italian, peso] of the individual elements gathered; their critical *reliability*, their respective importance, their (at least apparent) *truth* and correctness: is it right to say this or no?

10.323 *Discorrere* [English, to discourse] suggests "running [Italian, correre] (quite freely) here and there" through the material and thoughts which have already been acquired, with the aim not only of finding new affinities and connections, but also of seeing how the thoughts *structure* themselves almost spontaneously. It is a question of discovering the *immanent logic,* so to say, of the argument which is being constructed: if I make such a connection between the thoughts, does the discourse flow or does it not?

10.324 *Riflettere* [English, to reflect] suggests "turning back" upon the argument, beginning from the results already obtained, so that this argument becomes *better structured* in view of the results, and above all so that there are discovered the *lacunae*, contradictions, points which are not clear, jumps — which oblige one to revise and perhaps even to restructure the argument.

10.33 *Inserting one's own thinking, reflections and meditations into the discourse.* While reading and meditating on the theme there have certainly arisen quite a few personal original and creative *ideas and "insights",* which one will have taken care to note down on cards. The moment has now come to rescue them from the mass of accumulated material, to gather them and *reflect upon them, confronting* them with the more objective discourse already constructed. In this way the thesis can become a contribution that is really personal, without the danger of its objectivity being weakened by my preconceived opinions (or preferences or aversions).

NB: In view not only of the thesis but also of teaching and of further work, it may be useful to maintain a *diary* (which could even be a diskette), in which one jots down one's reflections as they present themselves.

10.34 *The result* of this effort of thinking will be the *thesis of the thesis*: a concise and precise formulation (normally a single and simple proposition) stating what one intends to assert and/or demonstrate, which up to now has not yet been attempted (not: "For St. Augustine God is triune"!). This thesis will now become the *working hypothesis* which will guide further research, and which one will try to verify, demonstrate, and eventually modify.

10.341 At this point it would be useful to draw up a *synthetic draft* of the whole thesis, explaining in *2-3 pages* what one would like to demonstrate and how, beginning from the actual state of research (and therefore from the formulation of the question). This draft will serve not so much as a sketch for the drawing up of the thesis, as a *private "witness"* against which to confront my further work, something that will give me the assurance (especially when I am in danger of losing the thread) that I have understood something.

This draft is also a useful basis for a *discussion with the director*, who must be informed about the progress of the research at this moment, at the very latest.

NB: Far from being a defect, it would be an advantage if the working hypothesis and the first draft are *lacking in nuances* and do not indicate all the material collected. In fact, at the beginning of the constructive phase of work, *sharp and simple formulations* which are almost caricatures (emphasizing for example the oppositions and contrasts) are very useful to nail down what exactly it is that one wishes to say. Otherwise, as the thesis is gradually enriched with material and the necessary nuances are added, there is a danger of sinking into vagueness and inconclusiveness.

10.342 Next one makes an inventory of *points that still remain unclear* and of the further research needed, noting: 1. what has not yet been understood clearly; 2. interpretations which are notably different from one's own; 3. (personal) assertions which one has not yet been able to verify or demonstrate;

4. all the lacunae in necessary information (historical, etc.). Before proceeding to the elaboration of the thesis (which in its turn will reveal other points to be clarified!), this further research must be carried out.

10.343 Finally one begins to meditate on the *plan of the thesis,* bringing it slowly to maturity, keeping in mind the following four aspects:

— *The order of exposition* does not coincide with the order of discovery (cf. 8.32 above). The latter was often casual and in a backward direction (the presuppositions of context, for example, are often the last thing to be discovered), while the exposition must lead the reader *logically and gradually* from the presuppositions and premisses to the conclusions.

— *The "ideal" reader* for whom the thesis is being written will not be completely ignorant of the matter, but *will already have a certain knowledge* and competence — one that is certainly greater than that which I had at the beginning of my research. I should not therefore lead him over the entire itinerary of my discoveries, which was necessary only for myself, to bring me to the level of competence which every *expert in the matter* normally has. One part of my preliminary research will therefore have to be left out and the corresponding material will have to be buried or "cremated" (as Harnack used to say).

— The *guiding question* in the elaboration of the plan will not therefore be: Where to put all the material collected?, but: What is the *minimum necessary* which I must present and explain to the reader, in order that he might *follow and evaluate* my argument? One must note that the quality of a book usually is in inverse ratio to its quantity — and this is true also, and above all, for a thesis.

— The primary concern however must be about the *clarity and logical coherence of the argument.* Even from a reading of the plan alone, one must be able to grasp the connections between the different parts of the thesis and the direction in which the argument is heading. The elaboration of the plan is a useful *check on oneself:* if there are assertions or necessary passages which do not quite fit in naturally into the plan, this means that the thesis is not yet sufficiently mature.

When the plan has been drawn up, it must in its turn be *discussed with the director.*

NB 1: In this short "practical guide", it is not possible to enter into the *particular methodologies* of textual and historical criticism, interpretation, speculative construction, etc. which the different ecclesiastical disciplines call for. These methods should be learnt not so much from books as from personal contact with professors, especially in the *seminars* of the second and third cycle, and from the personal guidance of the *director.*

NB 2: In point of fact, the elaboration of a thesis never flows as smoothly as described above. The phase of the collecting of the material itself often becomes an *intellectual "desert"*, that is, a period of great fatigue where one sees neither the results nor the meaning of what one is doing. The mass of material to be collected (or already collected) often provokes a *crisis of disorientation*: one can no longer see a way leading out of this forest into the light. When one finally arrives at the decisive moment of the thoughtful construction, one experiences such a *mental emptiness* that one no longer understands anything, or else one sees only difficulties and contradictions.

To get out of this state of crisis, one must take care first of all to *vary the type of work*. While studying the sources, for example, one could read some secondary literature which is easier and more reassuring. Most importantly, the gathering of material must be interspersed with moments of organization and of thought.

Finally, in order to overcome the crisis of disorientation and of blankness, it would be good to take a solid and prolonged *creative break*, a real rest from the work of thinking about the thesis. In fact, by leaving aside a determinate intellectual work for a period of time, one paradoxically gives it a chance to mature. After the pause one can get back to the work with some stimulating reading which is not directly connected with the thesis but is related to it. Slowly, one's "speculative imagination" will re-establish itself.

A similar but shorter pause is recommended between the first and definitive elaboration of the thesis.

10.4 *The elaboration of the thesis*

A good thesis, like any scientific book or article, normally needs to be written at least 2 or 3 times.

10.41 *A first draft,* rapid, fluid and terse, *without preoccupations* of accurateness and completeness, or of correct formulation, should provide a first text, which will probably be too loose and too long; still, it is something on which one can work. It serves simply *to put together and to put on paper* (or on a diskette) the essential parts of the material collected following the order of the plan.

In fact, if one tries to write a definitive text right from the beginning, one that is well constructed and accurately formulated, one will find endless difficulties; it is instead much easier to correct and re-elaborate an already existing text, however imperfect it be. (There are some however who cannot write except in "fair copy"; so let each one write as he finds best: each according to his character.)

In this first draft there is no need of inserting the notes; one could, however, make a brief indication regarding the note or reference to be inserted.

10.42 *Before writing a chapter* one should take some time to draw up a *sketch,* written on a large paper (the computer is no use here!) in a very *structured* and *well spaced-out* way, so as to be easily able to introduce additions or shift sections, and at the same time to keep an eye on the structure of the whole. It is worth "wasting" a lot of time meditating on this sketch, completing it, modifying it, until everything has found its proper place. Once this is done, it will be much easier not to lose the thread of the argument during the drafting of the chapter.

10.43 *To arrive at the definitive version* one must *review the text critically*, filling it out, making precisions and above all making it more concise. One should not indulge in merely making additions, and one should not be afraid of rewriting entire paragraphs and even chapters. In such a revision, two aspects must be taken into account:

10.431 Every single assertion of the thesis must be *justified,* by *referring back to the source* from which it has been drawn (this is therefore the moment of inserting the *notes*), and especially by means of *arguments and/or critical discussions* of divergent interpretations and opinions. The justification much be such that the assertions become universally *verifiable.*

If it is not possible to justify definitively some particular assertion, it must be explicitly presented for what it is, i.e. a *hypothesis* or a *probable opinion* (stating also the reasons why it is merely probable).

10.432 *The style* should above all be *clear and explicit and appropriate* to a scientific writing, according to the indications already given for the elaboration (8.23 and 8.33 above). A style that is too involved and language that is purely allusive should be avoided; one should say clearly what one has to say (and what one thinks). One should not be afraid to give detailed explanations if these seem useful. A thesis is not a political or diplomatic discourse full of insinuations. Its stylistic quality lies instead in its *rigor* and *conciseness*, which find expression also in the *sobriety* of the text. As a rule, the shorter the definitive text of the thesis, the better it will be, provided that clarity has been safeguarded.

10.433 *The notes* must be thought of *in the process of writing the text*. In practice this amounts to putting down brief indications regarding the notes while writing the text, and as soon as a chapter (or part of a chapter) has been finished, adding the notes in a form that is provisionally definitive.

References to Sacred Scripture and to Denzinger (DS) can be inserted within parentheses directly in the text, and the same may be said if there is a *single* work which is the principal object of the whole thesis, e.g. the *Summa Theologiae* (S.Th.) or *The Critique of Pure Reason* (KRV A or B). *All other references must be given in footnotes.*

NB 1: *References to one's own text* must not be forgotten (e.g.: "as we have seen on p. 87 above"), making sure however that all pedantry is avoided.

NB 2: One often comes across theses which are pure exposi- tions of the thought of an author, to which is added a final chapter (or a few pages in the Conclusion) containing some *"critical observations"*. Such a presentation, while acceptable in a licentiate dissertation, is an indication of *insufficient elaboration* of a doctoral thesis. On pain of remaining a mere compilation, the *very exposition itself must be critical*, clarifying what is obscure in the author, highlighting points which can be criticized and discussing what is debatable. To repeat once again: the thesis should not be an account of what an author has said, but rather a clear exposition of what the doctoral student thinks about it and for what reasons.

10.44 *The definitive version* must be entirely rewritten on the basis of the revisions mentioned above, so as to arrive at a text which is also stylistically *coherent and compact*. One who is constrained to write in a language which is not his mother tongue must make sure that someone competent in the language *checks* his text. Even otherwise, it would be useful to get some friend to go through the text, not only to discover typographical errors which have escaped one's attention, but especially to check the intelligibility and legibility of the thesis.

10.441 At this moment one finally adds a *Preface, the Bibliography,* and the *Table of Contents,* retouching if necessary the *Introduction* and *Conclusion.* The *Analytic Index* is prepared instead only if and when the manuscript is to be published.

The *Bibliography* should contain only those writings which have been used or consulted, and must always be divided into principal texts and secondary literature. Further subdivisions may be discussed with the director. General reference works should not be put in the bibliography, except specific references to some encyclopedia articles. In case of *doubts* about the *bibliography*, the following works may be consulted:

C.J. FUERST, *Normae scriptis edendis in disciplines ecclesiasticis.* Roma, P.U. Gregoriana, 1961.

J. JANSSENS, *Note di metodologia.* Parte prima. Rome: PUG, 1988.

N.W. NEWSON - G.E. WALK, *Form and Standards for Thesis Writing.* Scranton PA, International Textbook Company, [4]1953.

M. BLACKBURN, alii, *Comment rédiger un rapport de recherche.* Québec, Leméac, [5]1974.

R. BOUCHER – M. MIGNAULT, *Les étapes de la redaction d'un travail en bibliothèque.* Québec, La Pocatière, [9]1978.

S. PEREZ, *Cómo presentar un trabajo académico.* Guatemala, Editoria Academica Centroamericana, 1980.

G. BANGEN, *Die schriftliche Form germanisticher Arbeiten.* Stuttgart, Metzler, [6]1971.

For the presentation of the bibliography cf. also:

S. SCHWERTNER, *Internationales Abkürzungsverzeichnis für Theologie und Grenzgebiete.* International glossary of abbreviations for theology and related subjects. Berlin, Gruyter, [2]1976.

10.442 Before submitting the manuscript to the press or for definitive transcription, one must do the *cleaning up* or, as the French say, the *"toilette"*, which is a question of checking the *order and completeness* of the notes and of the *Bibliography,* the *uniformity* of the bibliographical indications and abbreviations, the *orthography* of names (especially foreign ones) and of rare words, the *correctness* of the texts cited, especially if in a foreign language, and *clarity and uniformity* in the divisions of the text.

10.443 *The final transcription* of the manuscript must be done with great care. All typing errors must be attentively corrected. The typographic presentation must be such that the pages can eventually be photographed for a publication in offset.

10.5 *The publication of the thesis*

For the publication of the thesis one should observe not only the norms of the University and the observations of the two readers, but also the *advice of the director of the thesis*. It is he who can judge whether it would be more suitable to publish, at a reasonable cost, an *extract* of the thesis in order to satisfy the academic requirements, or whether it would be worthwhile searching for a *publisher* (who possibly will insert the work in a series), so that the *whole thesis* is really made public and given publicity.

This will be the beginning of a series of other publications which the new doctor will not delay in preparing ...

NB: All doctoral students are recommended to read U. Eco's first bestseller, full of very practical advice:

U. ECO, *Come si fa una tesi di laurea.* Milano, Bompiani, [1988].

Many sane counsels for overcoming the moments of crisis are found in a book of a "Dissertation Therapist":

S. STERNBERG, *How to Complete and Survive a Doctoral Dissertation.* New York, St. Martin's Press, 1981. [This refers to the American context and to sociology, but has also a wider application.]

11. The use of the Personal Computer

The personal computer (PC) is a useful instrument for the

complex work of research and redaction of a thesis. It may be worth acquiring one for the work of the doctoral thesis, or at any rate if one foresees that it will come in use even after one's studies. If it is a question merely of having well printed elaborations and master's theses, it may be better to go in for an electronic typewriter with a small memory, which costs less and can be mastered more easily.

11.1 *Acquiring a PC*

Since the acquisition of a PC involves a substantial investment, it calls for reflection, information and caution. One should become familiar with the different possibilities, make comparisons, and listen to the advice of experts. Here we can give only some general indications.

11.11 *Distinguish between hardware and software.* The former is the machine, properly speaking; the latter consists of programs which are used in the *hardware*. Two types of hardware are useful for philosophical and theological work: IBM and Mackintosh. At the moment, these two systems are not easily compatible; inasmuch as the PC makes work in common possible (e.g. the exchange of information, of cards, of texts), this point must be considered well before buying the computer. It could be said (with prudence, because the technical developments are very rapid) that while the IBM was more advantageous because of the great number of programs available to it and the even greater number of systems compatible with it, the advantage of Mackintosh was its facility in composing texts; but these differences are disappearing today. It is not necessary to have the most powerful machine available, but a hard disk is indispensable; the current programs, and not merely the best ones, call for plenty of space; relying on a floppy disk would soon lead to many problems. In the same way, a RAM of 640 MB is necessary; the recent systems of expanded memory (beyond 640 MB of RAM) are very useful, but can be managed only by specific software.

11.12 *As far as software is concerned*, it is useful to have two types of programs: a *word processor* and a *database*. A program for passing from one to the other may also be added, e.g. from the file cards to the elaboration of the text (one could thus transfer a card to a note in the text). One also needs various programs which manage the machine itself and the hard disk, e.g. to recover texts which have been accidently canceled, to put order into the hard disk, or to discover and eliminate *viruses* (be very careful before using a diskette from doubtful sources, or for that matter, from any source!).

All these programs are linked to the hardware through an intermediary program (*interface*). Mackintosh has its own system; on IBM, the most common system is MS-DOS, the *Disk Operating System* of the Microsoft Company; all programs used must be compatible with the chosen interface.

11.13 The choice of programs depends on the financial and psychological investment that the buyer is prepared to make; there are programs which are both easy and cheap, but which do not have many possibilities (e.g. they cannot make indices); there are others which are very powerful but costly, mastery of which calls for weeks of learning. Some programs (especially those which use the "mouse") indicate on the screen itself the keys to be used in the word processor, while others provide a blank screen, which allows more space for the text. The more common programs in our field are: *WordPerfect* and *Word* (this is available also on Mackintosh), available in all the principal European languages, to which may be added *Symphony*, *Works,* etc. All these programs are updated every year, and sometimes every three months; therefore they are numbered (e.g. *WordPerfect 5.1*). A good word processor must have programs for correcting spellings, transferring text from one chapter to another or within the same chapter, searching for words, working on several chapters at a time (Mackintosh can manage 4 texts simultaneously), setting up indices, pagemaking, etc.

The programs for making cards are also numerous. The program which is at the base of all the others is *Database*, number III of which is still famous. *WordPerfect* and *Word* have programs for rendering databases compatible with themselves, such as *Library* of the *Perfect Corporation*. These programs make it possible to create different indices within a single set of records (names of authors, principal themes, secondary themes, principal authors studied, secondary authors studied, etc.), which will be very useful for working on a thesis.

NB: *Learning a program* calls for at least 2-3 weeks of training. If one fails to do this, and if one does not study the program well, one will have a marvelous instrument, but will not be able to make full use of it.

11.14 *The printer* is a very delicate instrument. It must be absolutely compatible with the machine and with the programs used. The nine-pin printer can do much, but the text produced is not acceptable for a thesis or a licentiate dissertation. A 24-pin printer is necessary. Ink-jet printers are also very good. Laser printers produce marvelous results, but are too costly for common use.

The investment must however be proportionate to the desired results. There is no need of a program which can make a name Index when one has to write only a licentiate dissertation. Nor is it the print-quality that makes a thesis valuable. A well-constructed text which has been typed out makes a better impression than another whose only beauty is typographic.

11.2 *The gathering and organization of material*

This must still be done largely "by hand," but can be greatly aided by the PC.

11.21 *For the bibliographical research*, whether preliminary and orientative or complete and definitive, it would be better not to rely (exclusively) on a *databank*, even if there is one for the matter in question. Databanks supply information which is too abundant, too uniform and too abstract to be able to *form a judgment* about the relevance of the book or article in question (unless they contain also a summary, "abstract", or at least an indication of the contents). "A book is not a title, an author, a date of publication and a publisher. These are conventional abstractions, indications which serve to find the book. But they define it rather badly"[3]. It is therefore more useful, at the start, to refer to the bibliographical tools listed in the preceding chapters.

Recourse to a databank (given that it exists) may instead be more useful towards the end of the work, so as to be able to include publications which are more recent or which have escaped attention. In this case, as in others, computer technology can exercise a useful function of control. But one should never forget that a databank is never more complete than the data which has been fed into it!

11.211 As soon as some information has been found, one must enter into the PC, in a section specially created for the BIBLIOGRAPHY, a *bibliographic card*, as complete as possible, assigning it a *code number* (so as to be able to refer to it easily) and other notes (relevance of the book, collocation in the library, etc.). Thanks to the "format" (different for books and articles), it is easy to have uniformity in the bibliographical cards (which is otherwise difficult to maintain). These cards will be useful for references to citations and will finally be inserted (electronically) into the bibliography of the thesis. If new data are found (e.g. new editions), the bibliographical cards can be easily updated.

11.22 *Notes and personal reflections,* drafts of chapters, research to be done, etc. can either be *entered directly* into the PC or else may be transcribed from "first drafts". In the latter case, their transcription is already a first step in redaction.

---

[3] C. POZZOLI, *Come scrivere...,* p. 204.

In order to maintain some order, it would be useful to enter them (very provisionally) under various titles of a INDEX (equally provisional) of the future work. One should be careful however not to multiply files, so as not to complicate the work of the machine. Still, it is a very useful thing to have the possibility of transferring these notes from one title to another, or to make copies under another title. In sum, the titles of the INDEX take the place of the files or boxes in which cards used to be collected.

11.23 *Cards from books read* may be made directly on the PC, whether by setting up a *specialized index* (cf. 7.222 above), or by writing a continuous summary (7.223), or by collecting useful citations from them (7.224).

11.231 If in the specialized index the individual entries are supplied also with the code number of the book (e.g. 021/293-295), the specialized indices of the various books read can be unified electronically into a single index, the entries of which can then be redistributed according to the INDEX described above (11.22). Without too much work one can thus set up a rich treasury of material.

11.232 *The quotations* must be transcribed with accuracy, checking them for exactness and supplying them with the code number of the book and page references. One should be careful to always *include the citations within inverted commas*: "...", so as to *avoid even involuntary plagiarism*, as for example when in the work of redaction one confuses the citations with one's own summaries, and even with one's own reflections. For the same reason, omissions must be included within parentheses: (...), additions within square brackets: [...], and one's own comments within double parentheses ((...)). Working on the PC it is even easier to make a confusion between texts of different origins than when working with handwritten cards. It is often more convenient to *paraphrase* the context of a citation than to transcribe it.

11.233 *Cleaning up* superfluous elements *from the continuous summary*, correcting it linguistically and inserting the appropriate citations into it (all operations which are very easy on the PC), it is easy to transform it into a true and proper summary, which can then be inserted into a critical review of the book (cf. 8.134 NB above), or into a chapter of the future thesis.

11.234 It is better not to use a *scanner* in the work of making cards — even if in this way one can avoid practically all errors of transcription. Apart from its cost, the scanner presents the same problems — aggravated — as photocopies: without having read a text attentively, and without entering into its *ductus*, one has the impression of "possessing" it just because one has copied it, just because one has its mechanical (or electronic) reproduction. More, while the photocopy allows the possibility of underlining the text in various colors, such a possibility is rarely available on the screen.

11.24 *To organize the material gathered* it may be useful to print it out, at least in part. In fact, on the paper one can embrace more lines at a glance than can be contained on the screen, and on the desk one can shuffle cards — physically, as in a game of "patience" (cf. 9.22 above) — in at least five directions around a "central" card: upward, to the right and left, above and below; all this is quite impossible on the screen. Once such an order has been identified in the cards, it will be easy to reproduce it also in the PC.

NB: So as to be able to carry out these operations, it is necessary to have delimited each card with an *obligatory page limit* already at the moment of entering it in the PC, and to have given it a *code* which makes it identifiable.

11.25 The PC further makes possible something that is quite impossible with files on paper: the possibility of *searching all the files* in which a particular name or concept is found (but be care-

ful of homonyms!). After having carried out a first organization
of material "on paper", it may be extremely useful to "waste" a
bit of time making such cross-checks and filling out.

11.3 *The writing out of the thesis*

The writing out of the thesis is greatly facilitated by the
possibility of carrying out corrections, big or small, at every
moment. The word processor thus combines the advantages of
handwriting (ease of making corrections) with the cleanness of
a typewritten text.

11.31 *A first draft* can be written *without preoccupations
of correctness*, without even having to look continuously at the
screen: typing errors, inadequate words, incomplete or long
phrases, punctuation, redundant or faulty formulations, etc. can
easily be corrected in a first re-reading of the text, after having
written some paragraphs or pages. It is not even necessary to
preoccupy oneself about the end of the line (if the hyphenation
program has been disactivated, the machine goes automatically
to the new line), or with paragraph divisions (which can easily
be introduced into an already existing text). To overcome the
initial block of the blank page (or of the empty screen), one
could begin by recalling the notes gathered under that title of
the INDEX at which one is working; one can then begin to
order them and insert them into a continuous text.

NB: It may be useful to mark imperfect expressions and pas-
     sages calling for retouching and completion, by means of
     some conventional sign that is rarely used (e.g. &). This
     will make it easy to find them with "search".

11.32 Despite these facilities, it is not advisable, for a scientific work, to write simply in a "freewheeling" manner; the
text would run the risk of deviating or becoming tortuous.
Before writing a chapter it is therefore necessary to draw up
(and here a large paper is more useful than the PC) a *sketch*

which is sufficiently detailed and which fixes the principal points of the argument. With this sketch (and with the material already printed out) near the keyboard, one can go ahead without risk of losing the thread of the argument.

11.33 After having drawn up a chapter (or what corresponds to a section of the INDEX in the material collected) in this way, one can improve upon it and *enrich it with the help of the material collected.* To do this, the material is called up as when required in a "window" in the text; it is examined, edited and inserted if useful, or else discarded. The discarded material — stored in the memory — should be examined a second time so as to discern what should be conserved in another file for future use, and what should simply be thrown away (i.e. canceled). One should not think of inserting as much material as possible into the text; here also it is *not the quantity which makes the quality.*

11.34 *A more accurate revision* of the first draft is better done *on paper* than on the screen, because more text can be embraced at a glance, and corrections to be made can be noted more easily (with colored pens). For this reason (and for reasons of safety) it is advisable to *take a print of the text as soon as it is written.* For corrections, it is useful to have a printout with large margins and with ample space between the lines. But it is neither necessary nor useful to justify the margins; a text which is graphically too perfect does not lend itself to corrections. On the other hand, the impression of strangeness which is had when seeing one's own writing in print, could make possible a more objective examination and criticism, allowing as it does a distance from one's own production — as when one corrects page proofs.

When transferring corrections made on paper to the PC, it is often faster to retype certain words or phrases than to make great shifts. But one must be careful to delete the text which has been substituted!

11.4 *The final 'cleaning up' of the text*

Without any doubt, the final cleaning up of the text is done better on the PC than on paper.

11.41 *One can check* not only the spelling (with the dictionary incorporated in certain programs) and the hyphenation, but also the uniform use of technical terminology (e.g. "computer" or "calculator"), the repetitiveness of certain phrases (e.g. "without a doubt") and the length of phrases (by making the cursor jump from full stop to full stop). In the same way one can check whether inverted commas have been closed (or opened), and whether spaces have been maintained after punctuation marks. The bibliographical indications in the footnotes must also be checked against the bibliographical cards.

11.42 With the bibliographical cards as basis, one will also draw up the *Bibliography*. The *Table of Contents* will be constituted from the titles inserted into the text; this will allow a further check on the coherence of the whole work. A doctoral thesis is not usually provided with an *Analytic Index* of names and subjects; but given that many programs have this possibility, it may be useful to prepare an *Index of names* — especially since this will in turn allow a check of the spelling of names, especially foreign ones.

11.43 The last operation to be done before the final printing is the *pagination*, taking care not to lose any line of text, nor to leave a title on the last line of a page, nor to leave the last line of a chapter on a new page.

11.44 *For the publication,* after the defence of the thesis, the text produced by the printer can be photographed for *reproduction in offset*, provided that:
— the letters are really black (not therefore printed on a 9-pin printer, or in draft quality);
— the pagination is adjusted, odd pages being on the right, even pages on the left (i.e. always towards the external margin of the future book).

NB: More detailed advice may be found in:

C. POZZOLI, *Come scrivere una tesi di laurea con il personal computer.* Milan: Bompiani, 1986.
C. DE FRANCESCO, *Guida alla tesi di laurea col personal computer.* Milan: Angeli, 1988.

CONCLUSION

Many will find these methods of study too complicated, and far from the real needs of life — suitable at most for those who intend passing their whole life in study and teaching. Is it then worthwhile to use these methods?

Such a question involves an error which today goes under the name of "immediatism": only that is considered really useful and practical which immediately appears as such.

With this one forgets the space of time (which is considerable if one takes into account the rapidity of changes, even radical ones, in our world) which separates studies from future pastoral action. One who takes as his criterion of choice only what seems immediately useful, runs the great risk of finding himself with empty hands one day, having spent his time learning things which have already become dated and useless.

During studies therefore one must first of all *gather a treasure which does not fade and form one's own personality.* More than the doctrines which one learns, more than the schede which one collects, this treasure consists in a methodological *habitus*, or in the capacity, acquired in study, to be able to master new problems when these present themselves. Such a capacity already indicates an autonomous personality, and more than that it constitutes that tenacity of character which the heavy labour of study helps develop.

If therefore it is worthwhile studying, it is even better to study well.

INDEX

INDEX OF BIBLIOGRAPHICAL INDICATIONS

INDEX OF AUTHORS

Finito di stampare
nel mese di Febbraio 2004

presso la tipografia
"Giovanni Olivieri" di E. Montefoschi
00187 Roma • Via dell'Archetto, 10, 11, 12
Tel. 06 6792327 • E-mail: tip.olivieri@libero.it